Erotic Lightning

Intense Orgasms & BDSM Scenes With Electricity

Eibon

Erotic Lightning

ISBN: 978-1-329-78128-3

The information in this book should be taken as entertainment, not necessarily as advice or instruction. The activities described herein carry inherent risks to health. A medical professional should be consulted before attempting any sort of electrical play.

Table of Contents

Introduction

Regardless of your experience level with sex or BDSM play electricity can be a unique addition to any intimate relationship.

It's not my intention to provide you with a guide that shares a great amount of technical detail about how electricity works. An experienced BDSM enthusiast who goes by the name Uncle Abdul, with his background as an electrical engineer, has already done that better than I ever could in his excellent book *Juice – Electricity for Pleasure and Pain*.

Instead *Erotic Lightning* will concentrate on understanding electrical play from the viewpoint of the average person who possesses little or no knowledge of how electricity works, but wants to understand it well enough to play safely while creating fun and exciting experiences.

We'll cover different types of devices and styles, some that send electricity underneath the surface layers of the skin, some that feel like they travel the surface of the skin, and some that were designed primarily for self-defense (stun guns).

Please bear in mind since I play with women this book will focus on creating scenes with them. The same fundamental rules apply to anyone playing with electricity.

Electrical play has allowed me the opportunity to play at anniversaries, birthday parties, and in cities from Anchorage to Atlanta.

I hope after reading this you'll create your own memorable electrical adventures.

Best of luck,

Eibon

Glossary of Terms

Alternating current (AC) - continuous and bidirectional flow of charged particles (+ and -)

Ampere (amp) – the basic unit of current in an electrical circuit

BDSM – an overlapping acronym that stands for "Bondage/Discipline," "Dominance/Submission," and "Sadism/Masochism"

Bipolar - an electrode with two connection points and two separate conductive surfaces encapsulated within the same electrode. This device can be used by itself since it completes its own circuit. This device can also be used as a single pole electrode when only one of its connection points is used. Also known as double pole

Channel – used to refer to the output point of a power box. Most power boxes have two channels, occasionally they will have one. One channel will, in a standard configuration, power one bipolar or two unipolar electrodes

Conductor – any material that has a low resistance

Configuration(s) - this is a combination of what electrodes are being used and their placement on the body for maximum efficacy

Connection Point(s) - the point on the electrode where the leads are attached. There are either one, two, or four of these on an electrode, depending on whether it is single, double, triple or quadruple pole

Connection(s) - This is the end of your lead that attaches to the electrode. There are two on each pair of leads. Both of them need to be connected in order to create a complete circuit.

Consent - when a participant gives their permission for certain acts to be performed with them. All consent should be informed consent.

Contact - In regards to all electrodes, whenever a space is created between where the electrodes are placed and the contact area (skin or muscle tissue), electricity will travel in between that space

Current – a flow of electricity which results from the ordered directional movement of electrically charged particles

Dermis – the layer of skin beneath the epidermis, it has a much lower resistance to electricity than the epidermis (50 to 2,000 ohms)

Direct current (DC) – current that flows in one direction

Electrode - any device placed on (or in) the body to facilitate electrical stimulation

Electrode(s) - electrical conductors used to make contact with a nonmetallic part of a circuit, in this case, a person's skin

Epidermis – the outer layer of skin

E-stim - This is the use of low frequency electrical impulses from a generating source delivered to an electrode or electrodes to enhance an individual's natural sexual response. It is also referred to as erotic electro stimulation, electro sex, electro stim, or electrical stimulation

Frequency - number of cycles or pulses per second

Hertz (Hz) – the basic unit of measuring frequency

Insertable – usually but not always bipolar, these are made to insert into the vagina or anus and deliver electrical stimulation

Leads or lead wires – the wires connected to an e-stim box that allow it to connect to electrodes

Negotiation - the process of planning an activity or scene with a person, explaining the details, and arriving at informed consent

Polarity - present in every electrical circuit. Electrons flow from the negative pole to the positive pole. In a direct current (DC) circuit, one pole is always negative, the other pole is always positive and the electrons flow in one direction only

In an alternating current (AC) circuit the two poles alternate between negative and positive and the direction of the electron flow reverses

Power box - this is the power source for the erotic electro stimulation also known as a generating source, ie. An ErosTek, ElectraStim, or PES box. It controls the low frequency electrical impulses being delivered to the body via the electrode(s)

Pulsed current - electrical current delivered discontinuously

Purpose-Built Box - the PES, ErosTek and ElectraStim devices are examples of boxes specifically made to use for sexual e-stim play. It is not a TENS unit that has been rebranded

Quadruple Pole - an electrode with four connection points and four separate conductive surfaces within the same Electrode. It can also be used as a single-, double-, or triple-pole Electrode depending on how many of its Connection Points are used. Also known as Quad Pole

Safe words – words established prior to a scene that establish limits for play (e.g. "Yellow" means "no more" and "Red" mean "stop immediately.") In electrical play safe words may be used frequently

Scene – the negotiated content and circumstances of a BDSM encounter between two or more people

Scorching – occasionally you will read cautions about how to prevent "scorching" or "hot spots." These painful sensations may be caused by too little lubrication, contact with piercings, or by not maintaining full contact between the electrode and the skin. "Scorching" may or may not occur under these conditions. Lubrication may help in some cases

Transcutaneous electrical nerve stimulation (TENS) - use of electric current produced by a device to stimulate the nerves for therapeutic (or sexual) purposes

Triple Pole - an electrode with three connection points and three separate conductive surfaces within the same Electrode. It can also be used as a single- or double-pole Electrode depending on how many of its connection points are used. Also known as Tri Pole

Unipolar - an electrode with only one connection point and one continuous conductive surface. This device must have another electrode used with it to complete the circuit. It will not work if connected by itself. Also known as single pole

Voltage – a measure of the difference in electric potential between two points in space, a material, or an electric circuit, expressed in volts

What Is E-stim?

E-stim is an abbreviation for "erotic electro stimulation." Also known as "electrosex," it consists of using a power source - usually a TENS (Transcutaneous electrical nerve stimulation) unit like those used for muscle therapy - in conjunction with conductive pads, rubber loops, insertable electrodes, or other conductive items to create sensations ranging from pleasurable to painful, depending on the intent of the operator and what they've negotiated with their partner.

Erotic electrical play has existed since at least the first half of the 1800's, when vaginal electrodes were created and sold for use with "Magnetos" – electrical generators that use

Magneto-Electric Machine.

permanent magnets to produce periodic pulses of alternating current.

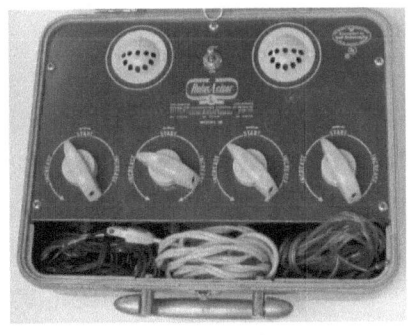

A passive exercise device similar to the "body toning" devices that are still popular now called the *Relaxacisor* (spelling variants included "*RelaxAcizer*") was introduced in the 1950's, using electric current to "work out" the muscles. It didn't take long for some Relaxacisor users to experiment with the device by placing the contacts on or near the genitals.

In the 1970's TENS units became more common and an unknown number of people around the world used them in an erotic context. It wasn't until the 1980's that the first purpose built boxes – TENS-like units that were specifically designed for sexual purposes – were introduced, namely the *Titillator* and the forerunner to today's PES Power Box, "*The Pleasure Box.*"

The 1990's saw companies like ErosTek enter the market and bring e-stim possibilities to a new level with microprocessor controlled programs, audio processing, and units that can be programmed with a computer.

How Does It Work?

The TENS or TENS-like unit takes a 9 volt direct current charge and amplifies the output while also boosting the voltage. This gives it the ability to penetrate beyond the surface (tertiary) layer of the skin.

The articles placed on the body where current is exchanged are called electrodes, and the current passing between the electrodes creates the sensations felt. Placement of these electrodes on the body determines where the sensations will be felt. Some who have experienced e-stim compare it to feeling as if they've been "fucked by a ghost."

Who Shouldn't Try Electrical Play?

This is the most important point in the e-stim portion of the book so please read it carefully.

The following statement from the ErosTek 232 user manual does a great job of explaining reasons to avoid e-stim:

"E-stim devices are NOT for use by or on anyone with implanted electronic devices (i.e. pacemakers, defibrillators, drug pumps, etc.), heart problems, heart disease, epilepsy, brain disorders, nervous system disorders, a history of strokes or seizures, serious skin problems or similar medical conditions. Not for use by pregnant women, women who might be pregnant, or anyone under the age of 18. Keep away from children. Current passed through the heart, neck or head can be fatal."

That last sentence bears repeating: **"Current passed through the heart, neck or head can be fatal."**

E-stim above the waist is dangerous. It's **not** a good idea to attempt any sort of e-stim play above the waist. You may have witnessed it done in videos, but if you play with someone with an undiagnosed heart condition it's possible you could kill them. Some boxes are sold with isolated channels that make them much safer for play above the waist, but realize the risks you are taking should you choose to do that.

Please do not try to use devices unintended for e-stim to do electrical play. It can lead to cases like this:

"CRALEY, Pa - A woman died during a night of "bizarre sex" in which her husband used an electrical cord to stimulate her, but ended up electrocuting her, police said.

Kirsten Taylor, 29, was found unconscious Wednesday night at the couple's Lower Windsor Twp. home. She was taken to York Hospital, where she was pronounced dead.

At first, Toby Taylor said his wife was shocked by a hair dryer, according to a police affidavit. But when burns were found on her body, police said Taylor told them he had clipped an electrical cord to his wife and plugged it into a power strip, which he then turned on and off." – The Patriot News, January 25, 2008

TENS Units vs. Purpose-Built Boxes

My first power box was an inexpensively-made TENS unit (sold by a company named "Zeus," formerly named Rimba) placed in shiny packaging to give it the appearance of an expensive sex toy. About two minutes after trying the sensations on my leg I made the decision to forget about the Zeus and spend the money to get a purpose-built box that was made for erotic purposes, the ElectraStim Sensavox. The

Sensavox cost upwards of $400 at the time but I don't regret the investment.

You may want to consider making a similar investment.

There's nothing at all wrong with using a standard TENS unit for e-stim, and if you have one sitting around I'd encourage you to use it after familiarizing yourself with the relevant safety issues.

At the same time there's a lot to be said about acquiring equipment designed by professionals to give the best results and that's what you will get when you buy a unit from ErosTek, ElectraStim, etc.

Equipment Reviews

Purpose-built units created and marketed for erotic purposes can be broken down into two distinct categories:

Analog – units that let you adjust the frequency, pulse, etc.

Digital – units that have microprocessors with programs, and occasionally offer other features such as sound processing that allows the stimulation to be driven by sound. They also frequently have knobs like ErosTek's "MultiAdjust" or ElectraStim's "Modify" which can change parameters (such as speed) of the built-in programs.

A sub-category of the digital units are **remote units**, which we'll look at separately.

It's difficult to compare the various boxes since what feels great to one person may not feel great to another, different people like different features, etc. but I've used everything listed here so will attempt to give an accurate account of what I've experienced with my partners.

The compensation I've received from these companies range from nothing to access to wholesale pricing in some instances.

Analog Boxes

Paradise Electro Stimulations

Available at peselectro.com
Retail price: $269.95

From the website:

"This little black box will put some 'spark' in your love life!!

The stimulation delivered is not so much a 'shock' as it is a 'tingle'. Nothing like the traditional mechanical vibration most have experienced, the sensations this Power Box delivers through the Electrodes have the potential to take your sexual response to all new levels!

The P.E.S. Power Box features: Intensity Control (Coarse & Fine Knobs) * Frequency Control (Frequency Knob & Fine Frequency Dial) * Pulse Control (Pulse Knob) * Two Power Interrupt Buttons * Two Non-Isolated Channels sharing a common ground allowing for easy set-up of 2-, 3-, and 4- Electrode Configurations. * The PES box operates with a 9v battery or 12v 1.5Amp A/C Adaptor."

PROS:

✓ The "tingle" mention in their ad seems to be accurate based on feedback received from partners. This box is frequently used by solo players who wish to achieve hands-free orgasms and it is easy to see why

✓ The power interrupt buttons are useful to tease and torment, it's too bad only analog units have this feature

CONS:

✓ The snap adapters included aren't compatible with most pads or insertables except those sold by PES, but the box uses a 3.5mm female jack for the leads, so inexpensive banana plug and TENS pin options are available.

✓ A lack of power has been cited by some users.

Folsom PSG-202 + Folsom PSG-MAX

 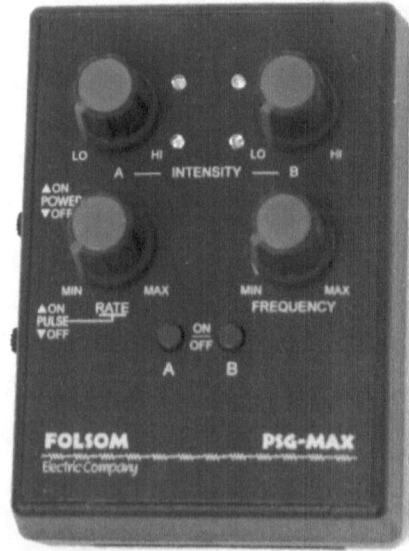

Available at huse.com and other online stores
Retail price: $245 for the 202, $345 for the MAX

From the Folsom website regarding the 202:

"The PSG-202 Pulse Signal Generator box is designed for those who are interested in sensual play. The output of this box is intended for sensual stimulation in the lower power ranges.

This box has two Electrical Output jacks, each with separate Intensity Adjustment knobs * Quick Disable buttons can instantly turn off either channel's electrical output * A Pulse Rate knob allows you to adjust the cycle rate of the pulse. Adjustment is provided from a slow long duration pulse to a faster short duration pulse * A Frequency knob allows you to adjust the frequency of the AC signal from approximately 15 to 200 Hz. This provides for an adjustment for both personal preferences as well as variations to optimize the output to specific applications * This box runs on a single standard 9-Volt battery * A jack for an optional external AC Adapter is provided to supplement and/or replace battery power."

From the Folsom website regarding the MAX:

"* This PSG-MAX box has two Electrical Output Jacks, with separate Intensity Adjustment knobs for each output. These output channels are completely independent and are electrically isolated from each other

* The two output channels always alternate their output. When one channel is firing, the other channel is idle. This feature has an interesting pleasurable effect as well as to allow safer applications of higher levels of electricity

* Quick Disable buttons can instantly turn off either channel's electrical output

* Green Channel Indicator LEDs (light emitting diodes) on the PSG-MAX let the user easily know that the indicated channel is either turned ON or OFF, and they indicate when current is being produced on each channel

* Red Power Level Indicator LEDs tell the user the amount of power being produced by each channel

* A Frequency knob allows you to adjust the frequency of the AC signal from a long duration to a very short duration

* A Pulse switch, when turned on, produces a train of "grouped" pulses.

* A Pulse Rate knob varies the group pulse length. When used with careful adjustment of the Frequency control, a quasi-random pulsing output can be achieved.

This box runs on a single standard 9-Volt battery."

PROS:

✓ The 202 box has a feeling that rides between the line of pleasure and pain

✓ The PSG-MAX is either loved or hated, depending on what sort of electrical sensations the user wishes to experience – if you like pain, you may like this

CONS:

✓ Channels are not isolated on the 202 so power weakens when both channels are on

✓ Limited functions don't justify price point of either of these boxes

✓ New design features an overlay sticker that looks and feels very cheap

Digital Boxes

ElectraStim Flick Duo EM80

Available at electrastim.com
Retail price: $239

From the ElectraStim website:

"A revolution in electro stimulation technology the ElectraStim Flick Duo not only has 8 built-in dual channel programs including escalating patterns but is also able to stimulate in rhythm with the movements of the control unit! Whether you simply want to add your own stimulation "beat" or want to stimulate in direct sympathy with your own wrist movements during masturbation, this patent pending feature will be like nothing you have tried before! The Flick feature can be slow or fast, soft or hard - it will mimic the sensation that suites your, or your partners, desire.

The Flick Duo unit has 25 intensity levels per output, ensuring satisfaction for all levels of play.

"Flick Feature"
Pressing the Mode button for 3 seconds will take you into the Patent Pending Flick feature. Simply make motions with the

control unit to vary the strength of stimulation but you still have control over the maximum intensity level. The Flick level is indicated by the 5 LEDs on the control panel but the output actually has 50 flick strengths! There are 4 different Flick Modes on the Duo Stimulator."

The Flick Duo also contains 7 programs: Continuous, Alternating Wave, Escalating Simultaneous Wave, Alternating Pulse, Escalating Simultaneous Pulse, Simultaneous Falling Rest, Alternating Dual Pulse, and Rapid Fire Escalate.

PROS:

✓ Unique "Flick" motion sensor opens up interesting possibilities for impact play and predicament bondage

✓ Motion sensitivity can be adjusted with four different settings

✓ ElectraStim offers a less expensive one-channel unit for solo players

✓ Rechargeable battery is convenient

CONS:

✓ Only 25 sensitivity levels for the seven programs don't allow for too much fine adjustment

✓ The "Flick" movement can feel odd to the bottom

ElectraStim SensaVox EM140

Available at electrastim.com
Retail price: $399.95 at Amazon.com

From the ElectraStim website:

"Create your own stimulation patterns by playing music or using voice commands to control the rhythm, intensity and duration of stimulation for a sexual experience that's truly customizable. The louder the sounds, the stronger stimulation feels. Independently controlled dual channels allow you to select different intensities to complement any electrode. Use up to 4 uni-polar or 2 bi-polar electro sex toys at once and lose yourself to the thrilling sensations only electro play can provide.

99 intensity levels make EM140 our most sensitive stimulator. As well as the audio-controlled options there are 9 pre-programmed patterns to explore."

PROS:

✓ Adjusting the levels up is nice and slow – the knobs must be turned four complete rotations before reaching the maximum level of 99.

✓ The "Boost" button is a unique feature and it makes for a lot of fun. Tormenting – and testing limits – is much easier with it.

✓ The "durable reverse printed polycarbonate overlay" really is durable. After approximately 7 years of use it still looks nearly new.

✓ LED display lets you know exactly what your output levels are at all times.

CONS:

✓ Although marketed in part for its audio capabilities the SensaVox doesn't process audio in stereo, making for "duller" sensations when the microphone and audio inputs are used, at least compared to the ErosTek 312

✓ The output levels automatically reset to zero whenever you change programs. This was done in the interest of safety and while not necessarily a bad feature it's a shame the user can't override it.

E-Stim Systems 2B

Available at store.e-stimsystems.com
Retail price: $399

From the E-Stim Systems website:

"The 2B has 17 modes. With all of the more standard modes present, we have added some new ones so you can now throb and thrust your way to e-stim ecstasy and pleasure. Split modes, tickle, and programmed wave functions all pack the 2B with hours of e-stim pleasure - and since the 2B is upgradeable, you can add new modes when they are released.

The 2B is fitted with the hardware for an optional digital PC link, which allows you to control your 2B directly from your Windows PC or Mac via a USB connection, and the free Commander software also offers computer to computer control over the internet.

The 2B features two completely isolated output channels, with independent controls on each channel. This allows you to use multiple bipolar electrodes at the same time, and be able to control them both, independently. The output LED's light up in proportion to the output levels so it's possible to see what's going on without consulting the main display. With the join mode it is possible to join both channels together, giving safety and control in one and with the Triphase cable set, even more possibilities are available. (Think 3D Electroplay)

Warning the 2B is considerably more powerful than many of the units available today - you have been warned."

PROS:

✓ Similar function to the ErosTek 312 but costs $200 less

✓ Processes audio in stereo unlike other smaller boxes

✓ Portable and lightweight, especially considering the features

✓ Ability to control through the internet is unique

✓ A lifetime guarantee is offered

✓ Online software is the best of any e-stim device I've seen

CONS:

✓ Some users have reported that several of the programs are uncomfortable compared to other units

ErosTek 232

Available at erostek.com
Retail price: $299

From the ErosTek website:

"A Powerful Portable!

Don't let its small size fool you. This dual-channel unit has a wide range of power and is perhaps the easiest power unit to get started with e-stim. It has features not found in any other portable e-stim unit including:

Designed and Made in the USA! * Audio to e-stim with built-in microphone and audio input jack. Sums left and right channels into mono. Endlessly expand your options via audio. * 2 independent output channels for amazing sensations. More erotic than other units which have a single channel feeding both outputs. * Intuitive MultiAdjust (MA) control provides real-time adjustment of mode tempo and frequency using a single knob. * 14 factory routines available: just turn the knob. * Special High Frequency (HiFreq) mode for low-level erotic stimulation (300 Hz max frequency) * Includes universal 100 - 240VAC adapter and 9 volt battery * 2 sets of 52" long leadwires with factory molded 4mm banana plugs * Bananas to Pins Adapters available to connect TENS / 2mm accessories * Small size (3.3" x 4.4" x 1.5") makes it easy to use and pack for travel * 1-Year ErosTek Warranty"

PROS:

✓ Built-in microphone is not only convenient but works very well. Especially good for voice and impact play scenes.

✓ Small size makes it easy to carry; it will even fit in a jacket pocket.

✓ The "MA" (MultiAdjust) allows for endless modification of the programs

✓ Price point makes this the best overall value in e-stim boxes in my opinion

CONS:

✓ The knobs to adjust the levels up are very sensitive. One must be careful not to go too far, too fast.

✓ No LCD or LED display indicating output level, aside from the blue lights that let you know when stimulation is occurring

✓ The ErosLink software that was supposed to allow the user to create their own programs never materialized.

ErosTek 312

Available at erostek.com
Retail price: $599

PROS:

✓ This is the "Cadillac" of electrical stimulation. The price is daunting but it is worth every penny. For over one decade this box has maintained the standard of "the best" – for good reason

✓ ErosLink software (which could be included at the $599 price point) allows you to create and store your own programs

✓ Stereo audio processing means you get the best available stereo stimulation

✓ Wide variety of built-in programs

CONS:

✓ For the $599 price a reasonable quality hard case could be included

✓ The size of the box is large, only because it contains a rechargeable battery in the rear of the case

Remote Boxes

e-play

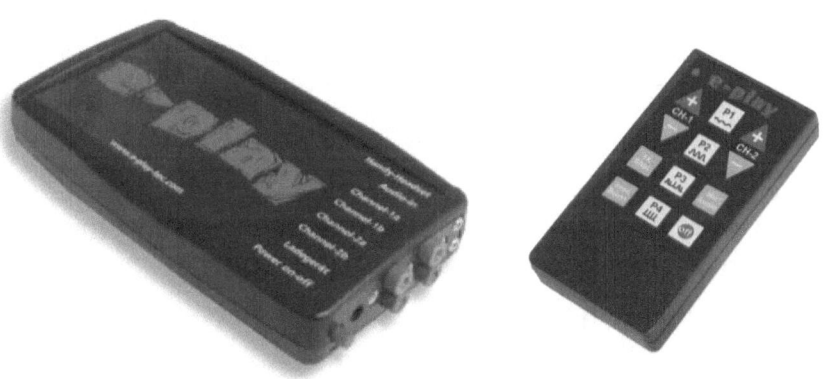

Available at e-play-tec.com
Retail price: ??? (not advertised for retail sale to the United States)

From the e-play website:
"The main unit EP-1 offers a lot of features. The unique pulse generator allows soft stimulation as well as powerful kicks upon your choice. Using the integrated microphone or the stereo connector the pulse generator will follow to the music. Two separately controllable outputs, rechargeable batteries, wireless remote control and even control by mobile phone offer a unique variety to the user.

Isn't it an amazing idea to take control over your submissive by a simple fingertip? The supplied remote control can be used very easy and the result of sub's reaction be viewed from a relaxed point anywhere in the room or even from outside the dominant has full access to his submissive.

The built-in NiMH-rechargeable batteries of the EP-1 offer power for 4 up to 6 hours playing depending on the intensity. The supplied charging unit is microprocessor controlled to provide optimal capacity and long-life terms. It avoids overloading of the batteries and fits to any wall outlet in the world. This grants fun during holidays as well.

Total control by mobile phone. Simply connect the e-play to your mobile phone and the headset to the e-play and get started. If you ring now sub's mobile you have full access to all functions of the e-play by pressing the keys on your phone. Of course you can talk to your sub through the headset as usual and hear the answers simultaneously. Just a hint: using a webcam will allow to watch your sub's activities...

Universal connection: Regardless of the slim size there are fitting connectors for the mobile, the headset, a CD player or similar. The electrodes can be attached to the 4mm banana jacks or the 3.5mm WalkMan sockets. Both channels offer both connectors upon your choice to grant a maximum of flexibility in attaching electrodes."

PROS:

✓ Phone control is amazing and a unique addition to e-stim play

✓ Power levels adjust up slowly – so slowly it concerned me at first, but it can be quite powerful it's better to adjust slow than fast

CONS:

✓ Bulky size for a remote unit, it measures 1 inch wide and 4 inches long

✓ High price makes it unlikely to catch on in the United States or elsewhere outside Germany, which is a shame – this unit deserves much more attention than it has received thus far

E-Stim Systems Remote

Available at store.e-stimsystems.com
Retail price: $269.99

From the E-Stim Systems website:

"We are proud to announce a world first... The First E-Stim Remote unit with a built in MOTION sensor.

If you are looking for a way to control your subject from a distance, then the E-Stim Series 1 Remote is for you. With a simple keyfob transmitter, and a powerful E-Stim receiver, the

Series 1 Remote gives remote control electroplay a new flavor.

Using a high quality digitally encoded transmitter and receiver (offering a range of around 150 feet/50 yards depending on environmental conditions), together with a dual microprocessor control system you can be sure that the Series 1 Remote offers you simple, powerful and highly effective remote controlled electro stimulation.

Key Features:

Digitally Encoded Radio Control With a range of up to 150ft/50yds

5 Modes including Motion Sensor & Training Mode

Keyfob style transmitter and small discreet receiver

Belt Clip

21 output levels over 5 different modes

The ability to link multiple receivers and transmitters

Safe biphasic current limited AC output

PROS:

✓ Price point makes it a good value

✓ Motion sensor can make for interesting scenes

CONS:

✓ No ability to stim with sound or music

✓ Only 5 modes

ElectraStim EM48
"The Controller"

Available at electrastim.com
Retail price: $340

From the ElectraStim
website:

"Control your partner's pleasure remotely... Perfect for Dom /
sub play * Long - range operation – up to 60 metres (200
feet) * User-friendly Transmitter and Receiver units * Multiple
operating modes * Microprocessor controlled * 7 Stimulation
modes * 18 Stimulation intensity levels * Boost feature –
Increases power temporarily by 25% * Trigger/Zap Mode *
Multi-directional, high sensitivity movement sensor * Audible
Receiver acknowledge beeper (can be muted) * Ability to
combine multiple transmitters/receivers * Leather belt pouch
* Conductive pads and batteries included

PROS:

✓ Only remote box with a "Boost" feature

✓ Trigger/Zap mode is unique and fun – it adds a layer of interactivity not found on most boxes

CONS:

✓ Intensity levels are limited to 18 (for comparison ElectraStim's SensaVox has 99 intensity levels)

✓ No ability to stim with sound or music

ErosTek 302R

Available at erostek.com
Retail price: $399

From the ErosTek website:

"Imagine a device that slips into your pocket and is completely controlled by a tiny 4-button remote control for portable, public, and BDSM fun. The ErosTek ET302R dual-channel remote-controlled power unit is the only one of its kind to offer legendary ErosTek routines in a small, easily hidden receiver / transmitter pair.

The power unit is small (3.75" x 2.25" x 1") and easy to take wherever you go. The transmitter is even smaller and looks like a car alarm keyfob more than anything else. Discreet? Very!

You get a 100% remote-controlled e-stim unit, designed exclusively for erotic purposes, by ErosTek, the leader in digital erotic e-stim!

Full Function Remote - Prevents tampering with adjustments for BDSM use * 10 Modes - Allows a wide variety of stimulation from erotic to BDSM training * Built In Sensitive Microphone - Allows creative audio-based stimulation * Lighted Display - Allows easy operation even in low light & exact settings * Glow-in-the-Dark Label - Makes for easy reference in daylight or night * Up To 100' Maximum Range - Easily covers most play areas * Compact Design - The main unit is small enough to be "worn" on the body * High Intensity - More intensity than TENS units and most competing products * Auto Shut Off - Saves the battery if you forget to turn it off * Medical-Grade Bipolar Waveform - Feels better and enhances safety * Highly Compatible - Nearly all erotic e-stim accessories plug right in * Multiple Remote Codes - Prevents interference with other units * High Quality Construction - Start of the art technology for small size and long life"

PROS:

✓ Has two channels unlike most remote e-stim units

✓ Built-in microphone is great for stimulating with sound

✓ Extra parts like the case and control are available separately in case they need replaced

CONS:

✓ Lacks a 3.5mm input for direct connection of sound/music

✓ Control can be confusing

Unipolar vs. Bipolar Toys

Notice that each channel on an e-stim box will connect to two leads. Only when electrodes are attached to each lead and placed on the body will current be felt between them.

For instance, connecting one pad to half the channel and placing it on the body will do nothing – but when another pad is attached you complete the circuit and the current will flow between the pads.

Speaking of pads:

✓ Don't attach them to broken skin

✓ Don't use them on more than one person

✓ Be careful to watch for muscle contractions once you begin stimulation with pads – if the muscle is moving too much stop stimulation

Some insertables may be triple or quadruple pole – that is to say, that have 3 or 4 contact points instead of one or two.

With a triple pole electrode you may split on end of the channel into two with the appropriate bridge cable, which acts as a splitter (available from several places in the *Resources* section), and connect it that way. With a quadruple pole electrode you can split both halves of a channel or use one channel to connect two points and another to connect the other two points.

E-stim Cleanliness

It's important to note that most electrodes used with e-stim – pads, insertables, etc. – should not be used with more than one person. If you use an insertable made of porous plastic and metal and someone's bodily fluids get on it, you won't be able to clean it thoroughly. You may always re-use it with *your partner*, but not others.

Pads and insertables containing plastic shouldn't be used on more than one person with one exception – if they're already fluid-bonded (according to *woman-health.org* this means "the practice of sexual partners who explicitly choose to expose themselves to each other's bodily fluids. Where there are exactly two fluid bonded partners, the term fluid monogamy is used. However, larger groups of people have been known to take part in fluid-bonded polyamorous relationships.") it's acceptable to use them.

Other insertables may be used with more than one person. Huse.com makes acrylic and stainless steel insertables that may be cleaned in a dishwasher or even boiled. Stainless steel devices that have been electrified, such as specula, may also be used with more than one person if cleaned thoroughly.

Variety of insertables from Huse.com – these are made of solid acrylic and stainless steel so may be cleaned and used safely with more than one person.

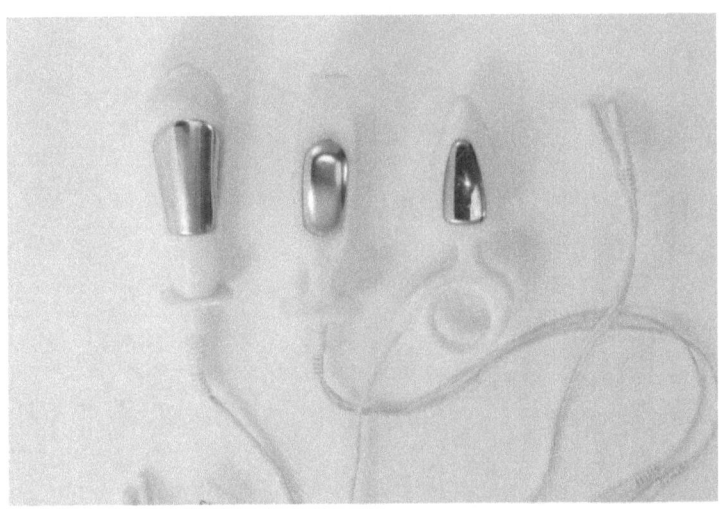

Medical-type insertables. From left to right – "Liberty Probe" or "Expander Probe," "Periform+ Intravaginal Probe," and an anal insertable. Do not use these on more than one person unless they are fluid bonded – they cannot be cleaned thoroughly enough to do so safely. Never use an insertable you used for anal play on more than one person unless it's made of stainless steel and cleaned thoroughly (e.g. boiled in water).

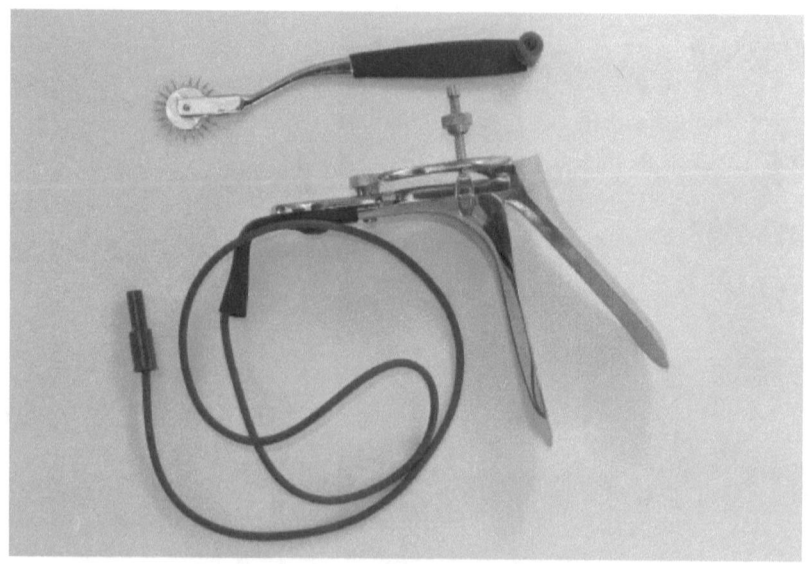

Wartenberg wheel and speculum. Note these are both unipolar electrodes. If using these together, one could connect the speculum to one half of a channel, then connect the wheel to the other half of the channel – current would only pass when the speculum is inserted and the wheel is applied to the body.

Connections – Banana Plugs, TENS Pins, Snap

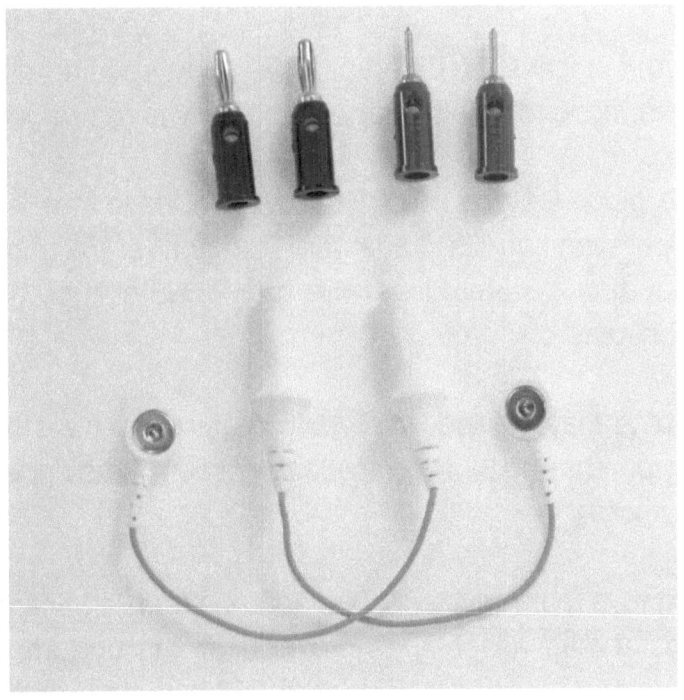

Top left: TENS to banana adapters
Top right: banana to TENS adapters
Bottom: banana to snap adapters

Different companies use different types of lead wires with their boxes.

ErosTek use a 3.5mm lead wire with male banana plugs at the end. The only e-stim toys made to use with these that I've seen are the ones from *Huse.com*.

ElectraStim uses a 2mm lead wire with male TENS pins at the end. Many toys and pads use TENS pins.

PES uses a 3.5mm lead wire with banana adapters at the end.

What this means is different toys may require different adapters, depending on what equipment you're using.

Banana plugs may be used with toys that have female TENS pins input with two TENS adapters (top right of the photo), or you may find a 3.5mm lead wire with TENS pins on the end to use instead.

TENS pins may be used with toys requiring a male banana plug by purchasing two of the adapters seen in the upper right of the photo.

If using toys that require snap adapters a female banana plug to female snap adapter, as pictured at the bottom of the photo, may be used. Or, if using a PES box, you could use a 3.5mm lead wire with banana plugs since the PES had 3.5mm inputs.

Also be aware that some electrodes that have the lead wire attached to them will need a 3.5mm -> 2.5mm step down jack to plug into your 3.5mm female input.

Sources for all these adapters are listed in the *Resources* section.

How to Do Your First E-stim Scene

For a first scene, where one or both partners have zero experience, it's good to start with a bipolar probe or two pads. One accessory on one channel is a good and simple way to begin. **Always remember to clearly negotiate your scene and establish safewords.**

1. Make sure the unit is powered OFF with the power turned all the way down before inserting or attaching anything to anybody. Also make certain it is off before removing anything later on!

2. Once everything is in/on, **slowly** adjust the power up while monitoring body language, breathing, and verbal feedback. Safe words should be established prior to the start of any scene.

3. Watch out for what is commonly called "scorching." This can occur when an insertable starts to slide out of the vagina – if she's very wet, or at a bad angle, or both, the insertable can slide out, and the edges or corners of these toys can give an incredibly unpleasant feeling. Piercings can cause this too, so don't attach electrodes to piercings. Different insertables often have different "hot spots" for this sort of thing. Once something is inserted or attached make sure it stays inserted or attached until the box is powered off. If it starts to come out / come loose **turn the power off immediately**, fix it, then turn the box back on at minimum power and continue.

Remember to watch your connections. I've had loose connections and the TENS pin has come right out of the insertable during a scene. If it does happen, turn the box off, fix it, and then continue. Don't touch the connections while the box is on or you may be surprised when you get a jolt.

Loose female TENS connections on an insertable can be fixed by squeezing them with your fingers or by very lightly applying pliers to them. Loose banana connections can be fixed by gently pulling out on the male connection to expand it, helping it fit tighter.

If the first scene goes well I'd suggest adding the pads to the equation for the next scene. Hook the pads up to one channel and the probe to the other. Attach the pads to the inside of the leg, near the vagina, or right above the vagina, and slowly adjust up. When you've touched on their limits with the pads, start slowly adjusting the channel with the probe up and see how it goes. **Remember to turn off the power box before removing pads, insertables, etc.**

Don't forget to adjust parameters during the scene using "MultiAdjust" or "Modify" or whatever your equipment allows in order to find the most pleasurable sensations.

After doing some basic scenes you can add in different insertables, more pads, split channels to use more toys, create music-driven scenes, and all kinds of other things - the sky is the limit. E-stim should be done in moderation. Try limiting your initial sessions to 30 minutes. Later sessions should last no more than 1-2 hours.

Some Advice on Orgasms

Women frequently achieve orgasm during electrical play. One lady claimed to have had a ten minute long orgasm using the ElectraStim SensaVox when we played together. But orgasms during e-stim – while common – are by no means guaranteed.

According to sex therapist Al Cooper's *Understanding the Female Orgasm* from 2003, fifty to 75 percent of women who have orgasms need clitoral stimulation and are unable to have an orgasm through intercourse alone.

E-stim attachments that focus on the clitoris are available and should be explored, but insertables can gain a great deal of effectiveness when used with vibrators or manual clitoral stimulation, particularly more powerful types of vibrators like the Hitachi Magic Wand. I've seen insertables literally shoot out when used with clitoral stimulation - if this happens the box should be shut off immediately as mentioned earlier.

It also bears noting that turning up the power when orgasms seem close can help put a scene over the top. As always, care should be taken not to go too far.

Sex With E-stim

One of the most frequently asked questions I receive at e-stim presentations is:

"How can two people have sex with e-stim?"

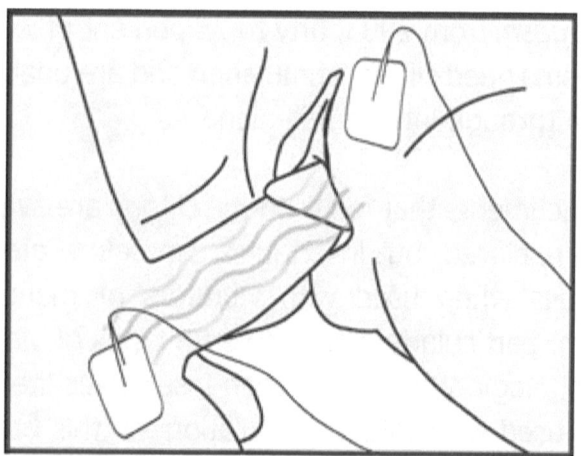

To do this use a single channel, then connect one pad to your partner and one to yourself. The illustration above (courtesy of ElectraStim) shows how this may be done safely. When contact is made with the above set up the circuit will be completed and sensations felt between partners. **Remember to keep all contact below the waist!**

A Warning - Anal Play

If using an insertable anally **never do so without plenty of lubricant**. Coconut oil, standard lubricants, or conductive gel will all work. If you fail to lubricate properly you could end up with your partner bleeding for several days – or worse - after the scene since the anus doesn't produce any natural lubricant like the vagina. **Never use an anal insertable on more than one person unless it's made out of stainless steel and cleaned thoroughly (boiled in water, for instance). Never place a used anal insertable anywhere else in the body.**

More Scene Ideas

One might divide e-stim play into two categories: **knob turning / button pushing** and **personalized play**.

There's absolutely nothing wrong with just hooking someone up to one of these boxes, slowly increasing the intensity, and approaching the scene that way. This is a great scene for any beginner to start and helps familiarize everyone with the equipment. I would encourage you to start with at least one or two simple "knob turning" scenes.

On the other hand e-stim is capable of facilitating far more intimate methods of play. Here are some examples I've tried, almost all of them require a box capable of audio-driven stimulation (e.g. ErosTek 232 or 312, ElectraStim SensaVox –

using MultiAdjust on the ErosTek or Modify on the SensaVox will adjust the sensitivity of the box to sound):

✓ **Conductive impact play** – using a box with a microphone during impact play, so that when a sound is made outside the body the e-stim is felt inside the body (or outside if using pads).

✓ **Hypnotic electrical play** – again used with a microphone and pads and/or insertables, hypnosis may be used to great effect. I wouldn't describe myself as possessing anything more than a dilettante's approach to hypnosis but strange phenomena have occurred that intrigue me and want to pursue it further.

✓ **Predicament bondage** – this may be accomplished in a variety of ways. I've purchased door alarms at dollar stores that attach to a door or window, then make a high-pitched noise when the two parts of the alarm are separated. The two parts can be taped to the arms or legs of the bottom. If the bottom is good at holding still and preventing any noise shoving or kicking their arms or legs apart can always help create noise. Again, a power box capable of audio is required for this. The ElectraStim Controller and E-Stim Systems Remote have built-in motion sensors as well.

✓ **Music videos, video games, adult videos, or anything else from a television receiver or computer** – Very inexpensive adapters may be purchased that allow RCA connections (the older type adapters we used to connect VCR and early DVD players with that newer high-definition

60

televisions still have) to adapt to 3.5mm connections. This means that with a long RCA cable you can input audio from your television into your power box. I've had women play video games and receive stimulation from the sounds of the game, had them watch their favorite porn videos and get stimulation from the moans and groans of the actors, and even had them watch their favorite music videos while "feeling" the music inside them. If using a computer for this a 3.5mm splitter may be used with an external speaker to recreate the same effect.

✓ **Reading assignments** – one of my favorite reading assignments for new submissives is Nancy Friday's "My Secret Garden." You may have someone highlight their favorite sections of a book and read it to them through the microphone – or have them read it to themselves.

✓ **Ambient sounds** – scenes that others are doing like flogging or whipping may be used to drive your e-stim scene while using the microphone.

✓ **Musical instruments** – guitars, synthesizers, drum machines, etc. can be used to drive the e-stim.

✓ **Sounds from the bottom** – using the microphone, one can tap on it to create stim sounds while holding it near the mouth of the bottom – when the bottom moans, yells, or makes noise the stimulation level is increased.

To end this section we'll examine one of the more advanced forms of personalized play:

High-End Electrical Play

"*Pulsating light and/or sound patterns have been used for thousands of years in almost all cultures to evoke emotional responses, from exciting a crowd to assisting in meditation to encouraging sleep. The techniques are part of folk knowledge, and science is just beginning to find out why they work. So as you begin to use light and sound stimulation you are embarking on a voyage of discovery and exploration.*"

- from the Photosonix Nova Pro 100 manual

A gentleman who goes by the name **Officer Wes** wrote of this "high-end" setup years ago. High-end electrical play combines sight, sound, and sensation play to create what some have labeled an otherworldly experience. Some look at this scene and compare to sensory deprivation, but it's closer to sensory overload.

3 items are necessary to do a high-end electrical scene, sources for all of these will be listed in the "Resources" section near the end of the book:

A sound source (this can be anything that produces sound – a MP3 player, drum machine, etc.)

A light/sound device (i.e. Nova Pro 100, David Delight, MindSpa)

An E-stim box capable of processing sound (i.e. ErosTek 232 or 312, ElectraStim Sensavox)

Optional: a massage pad that is music-driven may also be added (i.e. Homedics iCush Immersive Audio Sync Seat)

Whatever light/sound device you buy make certain that the lights can be triggered by external sound.

The Nova Pro 100 (pictured below) comes with the following warning, which applies to any light/sound device:

"If you, or anyone else who will use this machine, are subject to any form of seizures, epilepsy or visual photosensitivity, are using a pacemaker, suffering cardiac arrhythmia or other heart disorders, currently taking stimulants, tranquilizers or psychotropic medications, specifically including illicit drugs and alcohol, please do not use ours, or any other Light/Sound system."

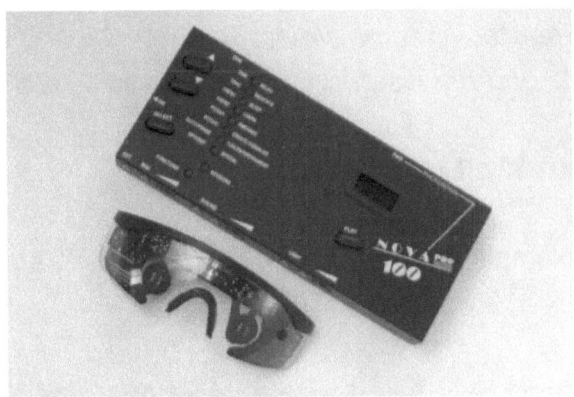

Nova Pro 100

This scene will work best with music that has a beat: pop, rock, rap, etc. Softer sounds will have a difficult time triggering the lights and electricity, and while the electricity can be adjusted up to compensate the lights usually cannot.

Some reactions to high-end electrical play:

"*Eibon's electrical play is fucking amazing. Lights, massage, current inside my pussy, and all of it set to music. He said it would take me to another orbit... um... hell yeah! I need to visit Boise more :)*"

"*I just wanted to let you know how much I enjoyed meeting you and how happy I am that I responded to your post! What an incredible experience it was... more and better than I could possibly have imagined. You were wonderful, and I don't know how to say a proper thank you. I feel so lucky.*"

"*I was completely deprived of my normal senses, but my body was overloaded with the lights, vibrations and electricity. As the tempo of the music increased, Sir kept turning up the voltage. I started to come almost immediately and there were only 1-2 second breaks during the entire 30+ minute scene.*"

How to put it all together:

(For this example we'll assume we're using a MP3 player with the ErosTek 312 and Nova Pro 100)

1. Connect a male-to-male 3.5mm cable from the headphone jack of the MP3 player to the EXT jack on

the Nova Pro 100 (this cable is included with both the Nova Pro 100 and ErosTek 312)

2. Set the Nova Pro 100 in "AudioStrobe" mode (press the arrow until the display reads "Aus")

3. Connect the glasses to one of the Nova Pro 100's LIGHT jacks (ColorTrack glasses from Photosonix, which change color according to the frequency of the sound, are especially good for this scene)

4. Connect the headphones to one of the Nova Pro 100's SOUND jacks

5. Connect a male-to-male 3.5mm cable from the other Nova Pro 100 SOUND jack to the ErosTek 312's "Audio" input

6. Make sure the levels are all set to zero on the 312, then turn it on and set the mode to "Audio 2."

7. Connect whatever accessories (insertables, TENS pads, etc.) to the 312 and your partner

8. Start the music and slowly turn the levels up until your partner can feel it.

Your audio source should be turned up to a high level so the lights and electricity respond well. Headphones with independent volume control are best, since the audio will be loud.

The Homedics massage seat I referenced earlier it has a built-in headphone jack with volume control and it's very handy. To connect the massage seat take the 3.5mm cable attached to the seat and insert it into one of the "Sound" outputs on the Nova Pro 100.

It's important to remember that your partner will have music turned up in their ears, so watching their reactions (breathing, flinching, etc.) is even more important than when verbal feedback is easier.

The lights on the ErosTek 312 (or other boxes) should be moving with the music – they shouldn't be too low, and they shouldn't consistently bright red. If they're too low turn the MA (Multi-Adjust) knob to the right, if they're too high turn it to the left.

Interview with Steffen of e-play (Germany)

Q: Hi Steffen! Thanks for agreeing to this interview. How did you become interested in E-stim?

A: This was long ago since I was thinking the first time about E-stim. Based on my interest in electronics I made my first early experience when I was about 16 years old.

Q: From what I've seen you are the only man in Germany who creates and sells e-stim gear like the E-play. What is the electrical play scene in Germany like?

A: For sure I am not the only one in Germany creating E-stim gear but perhaps one of the most sophisticated. The electrical play scene here is probably not very much different from other countries. Most people using E-stim devices are doing this at home and some of them also at SM of fetish parties. They very often start with TENS devices intended for medical health or muscle training and then find some more interesting usage in E-stim.

Q: What inspired you to create the e-play box?

A: The Germans are well-known as inventors of technical solutions or products and often try to make things more perfect. So did I after some experience on my own with stereo-stim. I was attending a couple of fetish play parties and therefore thought about an E-stim box with remote control and tinkered a first unit for my own. It seems to other party people that I had a lot of fun with it: Many of them asked me if I could build them a similar device. After saying "no, this is just a tinkered sample" for a couple of times I finally decided to develop a product out of this first sample and called it E-play.

Q: The E-Play is the only box I know of with a cell phone pass-through built in that allows the user to control the device with a phone. Was this a difficult feature to implement?

A: Since the remote control feature of the sample already was a big benefit on party playing I was thinking about an USP especially for couples that don't live in the same house. Using the tone dial technology it was not too difficult to implement this feature and is also easy to use.

Q: Could I ask what your personal "style" of play is with electricity? What sort of scenes do you create, which electrodes do you favor, etc.?

A: I think there are mostly two styles of play: One is controlled by yourselves and therefore features an E-stim box with a lot of adjustments, programs or channels. The other style is playing as couple where one of them controls the other. This needs an E-stim box that is easy to handle and reacts immediately upon controls. Nevertheless the programs or stimulation signals must be amazing and offer variety.

Using music as a source for the waveforms grants endless variety. However this works best in combination with fitting electrodes that provide a very good contact to the skin. The electrodes are responsible to allow stimulation of muscles or create tickling on the skins' surface. Since audio waveforms match better with muscle stimulation than with tickling on the skins' surface I prefer larger metal electrodes. They are also the recommended accessories for the E-play box.

Q: This is off-topic but I wanted to bring it up: you not only create electrical play devices but you are also very well known in the world of latex due to your VIVISHINE latex care product. How did this happen?

A: Latex has always been my fetish and can perfectly been combined with E-stim. To take care of the latex I was using a grease mixture that provided a nice shine. Funny, this was quite similar like the e-play box: My party play partner (Lady Vivian) asked me how I make my latex shiny. I promised her to bring her a bottle of my mixture next time. Just for doing a favor to her I made a sticker on the bottle and called it Vivishine. Then her husband and we have born the idea to create a product and sell it. The rest is more or less recommendation.

Q: What's in the future of E-Play Tec?

The e-play is not my main business but makes a lot of fun. Based on my electronic engineering business I am thinking about solutions that are small(er), offer even more variety, indicators or display, perhaps smart-phone controlled... If going this way it must be a long-term solution since I then intend to sell it worldwide and have to meet regulation requirements such as FCC everywhere. This is possible to do but of course needs time and money. Especially a sophisticated product in small volume production needs to be calculated over years of life.

Q: What advancements do you see happening in E-stim over the next 5-10 years?

A: There will be technical improvements as mentioned but maybe more important is that the acceptance of SM toys become more and more popular. Based on things like shades of grey E-stim might become interesting for more instead of being just a toy for kink people.

Interview with Anna at PES

Q: Hi Anna, how long have you been interested in electrical play, and what made you interested in it?

A: To be honest, before working at PES, I had never heard of electrical stimulation. I came into this job a complete newbie. And to be honest, for the first month, I found it terrifying. I don't remember now what made it click that it wasn't about 'shocking' but about a month in, I asked if I could have some product to try out. And it was amazing.

Q: Could you tell us about the history of PES?

A: I'm going to cheat on this answer. I've posted this story over on our new site www.danteamore.com. The link is here: http://www.danteamore.com/content/about_us

Q: The PES box has had more publicity than most sex toys – you've been featured on television from Canada to Italy, as well as on Playboy TV, CNBC, and HBO. What effect has all this media attention had on the company?

A: Well, it definitely helped us grow as a company. The Real Sex piece from HBO has probably had the most influence. Even now, all these years later, HBO still occasionally airs the segment and we get calls and emails. Most of these interviews have helped present electro sex as something that isn't just about 'shocking' or 'torture'. I think it has exposed a lot of 'vanilla' people to an activity that most of them would view in a negative manner had they not seen it in action or heard it talked about in a way that didn't present it as a purely BDSM activity. The publicity, for the most part, has opened a whole world of sexual pleasure up to people who might never have given us (or estim) a second look.

Q: PES is the only power box I know of that comes with 3.5mm to snap connectors – every other company uses TENS pins or banana adapters. What

prompted you to include snap connectors with the PES?

A: It was the low profile nature of the pinch leads. We started with banana plugs. They are big and bulky. Also the assembly of products that included them was a lot more complex. For example, the original PES Acrylic Penile Rings had the banana jacks. To protect the user from hot spots created by where the contact connects with the lead, we had to add something that provided some insulation vs simply directly connecting the plug to the conductive paint on the interior. The banana jacks also tend to be a little more easily damaged. Then there is amount of excess sticking up from your cock ring or out of your anal plug. Low Profile Leads make the connection point a lot more discreet and with an anal plug, make sitting on it a little easier. And with the move from purely acrylic products to our conductive silicone products, the low profile connection points were more easily molded into the product. Basically, it was more aesthetically pleasing; had better functionality and versatility; and it helped streamline some of our manufacturing procedures.

Q: Your store features a giant vibrating insertable called "The Samurai." I've never seen an E-stim toy that is quite like it. Could you tell us about how this was conceived and developed?

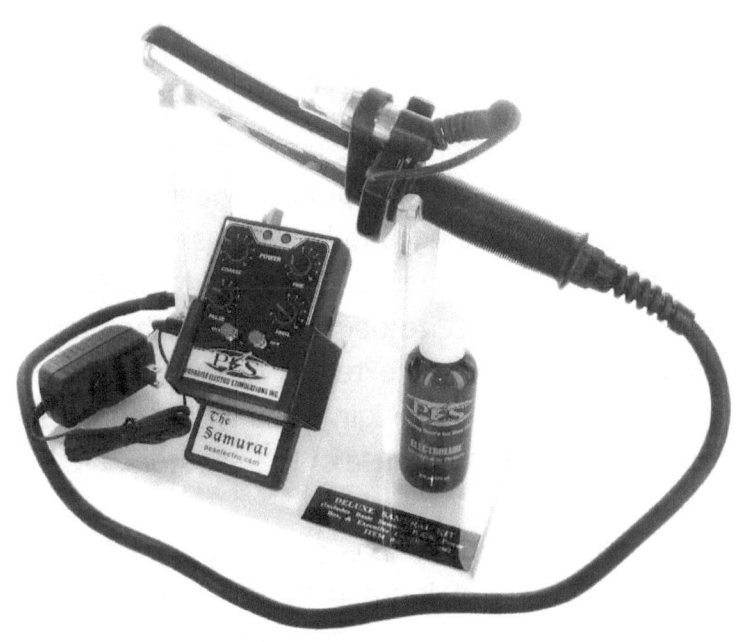

The PES Samuari

A: The Samurai was original designed as a replacement for on older female electrode known as The Juicer. The Juicer was a vaginal insertable with two contacts, similar to the Vaginal Plug, but it had a vibrating bullet mounted in the tip of it. When I started at PES in 2000, we were starting to phase these electrodes out because the vibrator was a problem. It tended to burn out too quickly and it was a bit of a nightmare to repair. Also, I asked Dante why on earth the vibrator was on the inside when most women tend to prefer clitoral vibration. So we started brainstorming a new electrode. The idea for the function of The Samurai is based on the classic Rabbit-style vibrator which would be the external clitoral vibrator mounted on the shaft, which instead of rotating would instead deliver electrical stimulation internally with a curve to aid in giving some g-spot stimulation. Making the vibrator an external piece not only made more sense from a sensation aspect but it reduced most of the burn out issues we'd been having because the problem was the motors in the vibrator. The insertable eggs we'd been using for years really didn't deal well with internal use. It tended to cause the motor to overheat and then seize up. Add to that the fact that we were wiring them up to an external vibrator control box that had more output than the original and we tended to see The Juicers for repair often because of the vibrators.

The shaft of The Samurai was pretty straight forward. We wanted a bit of a curve, it gradually increases in diameter as the shaft is inserted, and not so long that it would be too uncomfortable for most women.

A: Then we had to find a way to mount the clitoral vibrator in a way that made it adjustable to anyone's anatomy. So we made a removable cradle that could either be slid up or down the shaft to control the depth of insertion and also for the placement of the clitoral vibrator or removed completely so the vibrator could be held manually and applied with a little more variety for the user.

When the first prototype arrived, we were checking it out and our then manager said it kind of reminded him of a Samurai sword. We all agreed and so we went with that idea for the name.

Over the years since its release, we have made some updates but the basic design has remained the same. We tend to be perfectionists so we have made a few improvements to improve function & aethetics that most people would not be aware of but we are. We did recently update the Vibrator Control Box. The current one offers a little more variation in the speed of the vibrator than it had before.

I was the first ever user of the Samurai. I remember coming in to work the day after all excited to share my experiences. I was thrilled with what we'd created. The Samurai, because its contacts are on the right and left vs top and bottom, creates a feeling of buzzing or vibrating through the clitoral region. The internal muscles clench (and release) like most of the other internal electrodes do, but there is this added buzz that when you add in the stimulation from the clitoral vibrator is amazing and overwhelming. The bonus to the vibrator is that for someone who is nervous about electrical stimulation, is that if you start with a little light buzz on the clitoris with the vibrator, when you start in add in the estim, it can be a little less alien and startling for a beginner. It is kind of a distraction. Especially since a lot of first timers are nervous when they initially try estim. The clitoral stimulation via traditional vibration can help them relax a bit.

Q: What's in the future for PES?

A: In 2016, we'll be marking our 30th year in business. While we are always working to improve the products we currently carry, hopefully some of our other projects will be released in the coming years. We like to create product that is well-made and fairly easy to use, so sometimes it can take us a bit of work but we have some ideas that we hope to add to the line soon.

Q: What advancements do you see happening in E-stim over the next 5-10 years?

A: It is fascinating to see all the things that have come on the market in the world of estim even since I started working here over 10 years ago. Obviously digital and programmable power sources have been and continue to be the wave of the future. Conductive silicone, which we have been using for years now, continues to be a huge part of the market. Estim is still a very small part of the sex toy market. There are mainstream companies who have jumped on the estim bandwagon with cheap repackaged medical units being marketed as sex toys. I hope that cheap and quick is not the wave of the future as it has tended to be for so many other adult products. Quality product takes time and thought. Just because something can be electrified does not always mean it should be. Sometimes you need to think about the function and the form, not just how to make a quick buck.

Interview with Hella at ElectraStim

Q: Could you tell me what initially interested you about e-stim? What led to the creation of Electrastim as a company?

A: Andy completed a bachelor's degree in electrical and electronics engineering in 1999 after forging a career in a company producing TENs machines, among other products. He went on to work with another company that specialized in creating and programming pelvic floor exercisers designed to improve bladder control. It was during his time working with electro kegel exercisers that he had the idea of starting a company that produced erotic electro stimulation. He used his learned and applied knowledge to create a range of electro stimulators that were specifically designed for intimate stimulation. Over the years he's tweaked and improved his original visions to create a range of stimulators and electrodes that can be used in variety of different ways.

Q: My first "real" box built for play was your Sensavox unit and I continue to use it today. How did you come up with the "Boost" feature for this?

A: We knew that there was a strong electro sex presence in the BDSM world and we wanted to create stimulators that better reflected the games people wanted to play, Those using electro stimulators during fetish play tend to have the most demanding requirements, desiring a wider range of control options and a broader range of power levels. We therefore added the boost feature to our SensaVox and The Controller stimulators to specifically cater for this market. Boost can be used to push someone over the edge during a tease and denial session and can also be used to punish a disobedient sub. It's a nice addition to the other stimulation modes we've included in our premium stimulators.

Q: Not to reveal your trade secrets, but could you share some information about how the Sensavox processes audio?

A: It's not a huge secret, it works quite similarly to a set of speakers. The music device/laptop feeds an audio signal into the stimulator via the audio cable, where it passes through a modulator and into a power converter. The power converter then sends the signal out as an electrostimulation current.

Q: The "Flick" and "Flick Duo" are among the most unique e-stim toys I've seen since they allow the user to effect the stimulation by moving the box around. What gave you the idea to do this?

A: Our customers told us that they wanted stimulation to match their own movements for a more synchronized experience. This was particularly true for men who wanted to match their stroking rhythm with sympathetic stimulation.

We first added motion-sensitive stimulation to The Controller and found it very successful, but many didn't want the other functions that are more popular with D/s and remote play. Managing a separate receiver and controller when you're playing solo can also be tricky, it's easier to have a small handheld unit to take the faff out of play.

We'd been planning to make a rechargeable stimulator for a while and we decided that motion-activated stimulation would make a great addition to the smaller unit size that a rechargeable battery allows for. Because Flick and Flick Duo are both so small and slimline (smaller than a mobile/cell phone), it's easy to strap one to the back of your hand for that immersive stroking and stimming experience.

Q: On a similar note "The Controller" features a "Movement Sensing Mode" - one of the best features I've seen on a remote box. How did you manage to incorporate this feature into "The Controller?"

A: To sound a little cheeky, we simply added the necessary bits to the receiver unit. ;) The transmitter control sends an operation signal to a microprocessor which feeds the signal through to a motion sensor which connects to a voltage converter that feeds out the electrostimulation signal.

The motion sensor in the Controller receiver is not like other motion sensitive devices on the market. We use a super-sensitive omni-directional active sensor which means that the feature will work in any orientation with the same high sensitivity and will detect motion in any direction. Other devices simply use a tilt-switch or rolling ball type sensor which gives very limited one dimensional results, enabling the sub to easily trick the system. Another great advantage of the Controller system is that the transmitter has a display showing the "Controlling" Dom exactly what the stimulation intensity is and which pattern or mode is active.

Q: What is in the future for Electrastim?

We have a lot of new things coming up and plenty of ideas in the pipeline to keep our product range fresh and exciting. Our next big task is overhauling our .com site to bring it in line with our .co.uk domain. We're spending a lot of time focusing on education and information at the moment to help our retailers, customers and prospective customers learn more about the capability of our products and better understand how it feels to use them.

Q: What advancements do you see happening in e-stim over the next 5-10 years?

A: We have a lot of good ideas that we're trying out but they're staying under wraps. One thing we can say for certain is that erotic electrostimulation is getting more of a look-in with sex toy fans in general. With EES becoming more and more popular, we're expecting to see electro sex toys move away from being a strictly BDSM product, with more of a focus on the pleasure-giving properties they have to offer.

Erostek Interview (Anonymous)

Q: Thanks for taking the time to answer some questions. Could you tell us about your background, and how you got interested in electrical play?

A: I've been interested in E-stim since around puberty and I was also interested in electronics at that time leading to some experimentation. It's something I discovered entirely on my own. It wasn't until years later I learned others enjoyed it as well. As they say, one thing eventually led to another.

Q: Your ErosTek 212 box came out in 1998 (or was it 1999?) and was years ahead of its time with audio capabilities and a built-in microphone. Could you give us a timeline of the various boxes ErosTek has created, along with their distinctive features?

A: The first Erostek product was the ET201R first generation remote unit. It was designed in 1998 and, at the time as far anyone knows, was the first microprocessor controlled digital E-stim unit made for erotic use in the world. Prior to ErosTek there were only analog erotic units like the PES Power Box, two models from Folsom Electric and some other really simple designs. Other devices were made for medical use, muscle stimulation, animal training, etc. The ET201R was designed for low volume manufacturing and used almost entirely off-the-shelf components.

The ET201R was also the first true symmetrical bipolar erotic E-stim device. To this day most of the competition uses an asymmetrical pulse waveform which is less expensive but has some inherent disadvantages and even potential safety concerns. All ErosTek devices push and pull the current equally in both directions. Most E-stim units made for erotic use, and the inexpensive medical "knock off" units, push much higher levels of current in one direction. One possible side effect from a non-symmetrical waveform is migration of electrode materials, lubricants, conductive gels, etc. into the body through processes such as electrophoresis. This is especially a concern using electrodes that contain toxic metals and materials as many do.

The ET212 soon followed in 1999 and was designed as a significant upgrade from the Folsom and PES units. It was the predecessor to the current ET232. It was very well received and, like the ET201R, used a microprocessor to greatly expand the variety of stimulation. It also introduced the concept of Multi-Adjust to allow adjusting different parameters with different modes. Like the ET201R, it was also designed for low volume manufacturing.

The ET312 was born in 2002 as essentially a high-end cost-no-object design and pioneered many firsts for erotic E-stim:

- First to use a digital display providing feedback and accurate repeatable adjustments.

- First to use a large rechargeable battery enabling higher pulse frequencies, higher power levels, and much longer battery life. The higher power output circuitry allowed new kinds of stimulation previously impossible from units powered by small batteries.

- First with a digital interface and optional PC software allowing expanded computer control and added stimulation routines.

- First to incorporate stereo 2 channel audio opening up a new world of audio-based stimulation--including third party software such as SmartStim.

- First allowing two units to be linked together for coordinated 4 channel stimulation.

- And many more unique features like an external microphone, multiple power ranges, advanced adjustment menus, etc.

The ET302R was designed as a significant upgrade from the earlier ET201R remote unit and debuted in 2003. The ET302R was the first erotic E-stim unit to use surface mount technology allowing more functionality to be packed into a smaller device. Compared to its predecessor, it adds a more powerful microprocessor, digital display, a second channel, more advanced remote control, and several other enhancements. It was also designed to be made in higher volumes using automated assembly techniques.

The ET232 was similarly designed as a significant upgrade from the ET212 and came out in 2004. It also uses surface mount technology, higher quality components, a more advanced microprocessor, and many other enhancements. It and the ET312 have become the most popular erotic E-stim devices in the world. You only have to look at E-stim photos on fetish sites and you'll see more ErosTek devices than any other manufacture by a wide margin.

Q: The ET-312 has been around for years and is still considered the absolute best. In your opinion why is that?

A: Why is the ET312 still so popular? I think it's partly reputation. People really like them. It's also still the only true high-end design. Even the much newer products from E-stim

Systems, Electrastim, etc, are designed to be inexpensive to produce. They use 9 volt batteries which limit their capabilities, have a short battery life, and lack many of the ET312's more advanced features. Most of them don't even have a symmetrical bipolar output. Many competing products are also not as nice to use.

Q: It's been said that the ET-312 uses DSP (digital signal processing) with its audio input in order to provide a smoother experience. Could you explain how this works?

A: You can say the ET312 uses DSP for the audio processing but it's not the sort of DSP that is typically used in the audio world. The audio is being sampled, digitized, and converted into an E-stim waveform designed for the human body. That's done in real time with very little delay so, with music, the beat of the music you hear will be in sync with the stimulation.

This business has some substantial product liability issues and risks. It also requires a lot of customer service and customer education. And the products are made in much lower volumes than typical consumer electronics which presents many challenges.

Q: What's the most challenging aspect of running Erostek?

A: The relatively low sales volume greatly increases the manufacturing costs, requires amortizing the development costs over a much smaller number of units, and limits the number of custom made-to-order components that are practical. Nearly everything about, say an iPod, is designed just for that device. They use custom microprocessors (Systems On A Chip), custom displays, custom enclosures, etc. The one-time costs to design, tool up, test, and manufacture those custom components easily runs well into the six figures for just a single product. So, including the other development costs (hardware design, firmware, prototypes, etc.) Apple could easily be in the red a million+ dollars before they ship their first new iPod. But their sales volumes are so high, they quickly recover those costs and start turning a profit. That's not possible with a niche low-volume product like erotic E-stim devices.

The above is why it's not fair to compare say an ET232 to an iPod. Mainstream consumer electronics establish expectations for consumers that simply can't be met with a product that sells in drastically lower volumes yet must still be semi-affordable.

Q: What do you see in the future for ErosTek?

A: ErosTek is working on multiple new products but we're not discussing them at this time. We've learned the hard way people stop buying your existing products if you tempt them with what's around the corner. As far as I know, our products, despite being older, are still outselling the competition. That said, we acknowledge we have more competition than we used to and there have been many significant new trends with consumer electronics. We're working on next generation products but, for obvious reasons, we're not discussing the timeline or details just yet.

It's also worth pointing out we do periodically update and improve our existing products. The ET312, for example, just had some revisions made with a new enclosure, panel graphics, and some minor hardware updates. When we identify something like a durability issue, for example, we try to address it with product improvements. Many of these are all but invisible to most customers.

Q: What advances do you see happening in E-stim over the next 5-10 years?

A: I don't think anyone has a crystal ball for the future of E-stim. There were a lot of predictions 5 and 10 years ago, for example, that have not become reality. One of those was widespread adoption of using E-stim for various forms of online "cybersex." When you take what's already a niche product, and split out a small subset of that niche, you're left with a very small pool of customers. It makes a lot of things commercially impractical however appealing they might seem to a select few.

If you look at a product like the DreamLover 2000* it seems innovative at first, and then you realize the entire premise is easily defeated with a bit of kitchen plastic wrap tucked under the electrodes with a finger. Many like to dream big when it comes to E-stim, but the realities are often very different.

We certainly have an opinion about what future products from ErosTek will look like and how they'll incorporate much newer technology but we're not disclosing any of that yet for the reasons mentioned above. Several advances have enabled new paradigms for E-stim. We hope to continue to as the leader in the industry.

* *The DreamLover 2000 is a remote controlled male chastity E-stim device, available at dreamloverlabs.com*

The Violet Wand

Originally known as the "violet ray" and produced as an electrotherapy device in the early 1900's, the violet wand is used to apply low current, high voltage (usually a minimum of 35 kV to a maximum of 65 kV), high-frequency electricity to the body.

The sensation is often described as similar to "static" electricity (it's not – it's electromagnetic energy, but very similar to static) and feels as if it travels the surface of the skin, unlike the electricity generated by a TENS unit which creates sensations under the skin. When there is a small amount of space in between the wand electrode and anything conductive (skin, metal, etc.) the electricity will arc to the conductive surface. Since it's electricity it will always follow the path of least resistance.

The basic design for the violet wand was created by Nikola Tesla in the late 1800's. Violet rays were marketed as health devices that could cure everything from baldness to headaches.

Starting in 1951 the U.S. Food and Drug Administration sued manufacturers for making "false and misleading" medical claims, which brought an end to that style of marketing.

From the 1970's through the 80's a Chicago Police Detective Jon Burge allegedly used a violet ray to torture suspects. Years later Burge was convicted of two counts of obstruction of justice and one count of perjury and served 4.5 years in jail, but was never specifically convicted of torture since the statute of limitations had expired.

The more elaborate kits included many electrodes (glass attachments) designed to treat a variety of ailments, like this "Renulife" set:

Safety Concerns

✓ Don't use the violet wand on anyone with a pacemaker, insulin pump, or other electric implant

✓ Don't use the wand on anyone with a history of nerve damage or heart disease. It could disrupt the electrical impulses of an unstable heart

✓ Keep away from water

✓ The violet wand can ignite flammable liquids – unless you're doing fire play, keep it away from alcohol and other flammable liquids

✓ The wand arcs to metal, so watch out for piercings – you can use it on piercings, but use it sparingly, especially at first

✓ Don't use the wand in conjunction with any other form of electrical play. It can fry electronics, so keep your e-stim boxes, cell phones, and other electronics away from it

✓ The general rule is: the larger the contact surface of an electrode the milder the sensation, the smaller (or pointier) the contact surface of the electrode the more intense the sensation. E.g. it's good to start a scene with a round light bulb or mushroom probe, whereas a small metal pick can be used for violet wand branding

✓ Don't use the wand on the same area of the body for too long. Redness occurs often, is normal, and should fade in a few days. If used too long it can cause a sunburn like effect

✓ If using the wand near the face make sure contact lenses / glasses are removed so the electricity doesn't arc to them – **keep electricity away from eyes**

✓ Don't use the wand on someone for more than 10-15 minutes until you have some idea how they will react to it

✓ If using an extension cord make sure it can handle the power going through it

✓ Ensure electrodes are firmly in the base of the generator – otherwise you could get painful arcs or the electrode could fall out and break

✓ Watch the base of the wand where the electrode is inserted – if you get this too close to your partner the sparks may jump from the base directly to them

How to Buy a Violet Wand

Several companies sell violet wands online but it may be a better idea to put together a kit yourself depending on what you wish to do.

Let's go over the essential components of a functional violet wand kit:

The Generator

The standard violet wand generator included in many kits for sale online is called the *BD-10A High Frequency Generator.* Used to test neon sign equipment, it's manufactured and sold by a company named Electro-Technic Products, Inc. and their website is available in the "Resources" section. At the time of this writing the price is $211.

Despite claims to the contrary by some violet wand merchants who want to seem mysterious it doesn't look like they make any modifications to the BD-10A, aside from adding their name plate or other cosmetic changes. Also, any arguments you hear about "wax core" vs. "ceramic core" are meaningless when talking about wands of recent vintage.

The "core" is actually referring to the capacitor – wands don't really have a "core."

My personal advice would be to purchase a BD-10A instead of one of the lower-priced "neon" or "twilight" wands. Also known as "solid state" wands (the BD-10A and older models are called "mechanical wands"), these are relabeled beauty devices that have nowhere near the power of a BD-10A. The BD-10A will operate at approximately seven times the wattage of a solid state wand. The solid state wands are inexpensive so you may want to try one to see what they're like, but they are not indicative of the power you would expect from a mechanical wand.

There is another model sold by Electro Technic called the *BD-10AS*. The "S" in "*10AS*" stands for "switch" since it has a built-in switch that turns the wand on when pressed. I don't recommend this model since it won't work properly with a foot switch.

Body Contact Probe

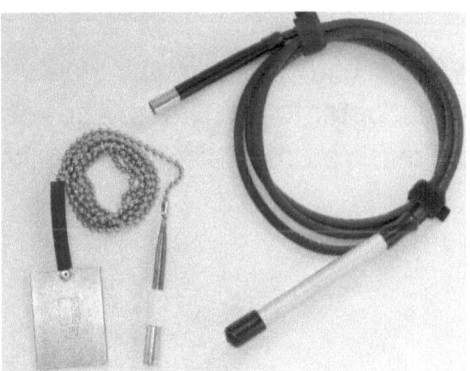

The body contact probe is the most important accessory you can own. Without it the "direct" and "indirect" techniques mentioned in the next few pages are impossible. The probe

93

in the photo on the left is from Rupert Huse & Son, the one on the right is similar to a probe sold by violetwands.com.

Only use body contact probes that are "spark gapped" – these halt household current.

Edison Adapter

The Edison Adapter allows you to use any standard base light bulb as a wand electrode. Large, round bulbs should create a milder sensation, while bulbs with a point (e.g. "flicker flame" candelabra-base bulbs) will be more intense.

Even bulbs that are burnt out will still work. You'll want to get a candelabra adapter to use with this so you're able to use smaller-base bulbs. You may also use a splitter to use two bulbs at once.

Footswitch

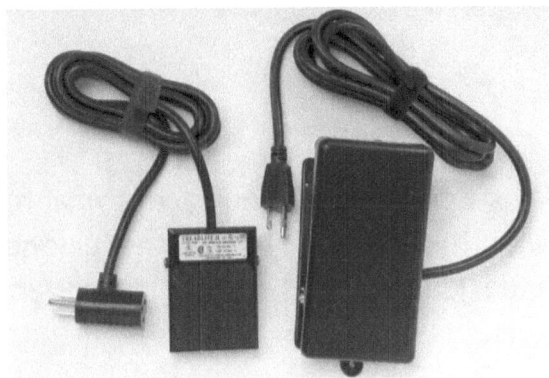

Using a footswitch lets you operate the wand hands free – the wand plugs into the switch, and the switch plugs into the wall. You can then set the wand to the power you desire and it will only turn on when the switch is pressed.

The switch on the left is a Treadlite II sold by Huse.com and available many other places. The switch on the right is a generic "Momentary Power Foot Switch" sold by Harbor Freight. I prefer the Harbor Freight switch even though it's more bulky, because it's better insulated. If using a Treadlite II switch make sure to wear shoes while doing so, otherwise your foot will feel the spark of the wand.

Three Ways to Play with the Violet Wand

There are three techniques that you may use with a violet wand. They are:

Direct Technique

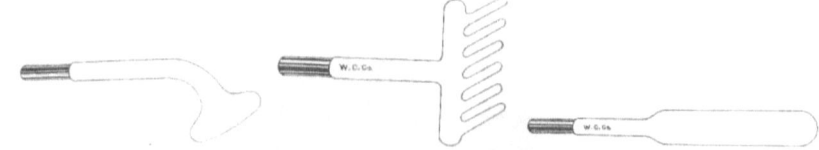

This is the most common technique and is what many people associate with the wand. It involves placing an glass electrode in the generator and applying the current through it to your partner.

The electrodes pictured above (from left: mushroom, rake, probe) are included in many violet wand kits. Edison adapters with light bulbs may also be used.

Indirect Technique

Indirect requires the use of a body contact probe. The probe is placed against your body, allowing the current to travel from you to your partner.

Anything conductive that you hold at this point will become a violet wand implement. Forks, knives, a wire coat hanger, etc.

Reverse Technique

The reverse technique is similar to indirect, the only difference being that the body contact probe is placed against the body of the person on the receiving end. The sensation has been described as "feeling it from the inside out." This technique is advantageous in that it allows for the greatest freedom of movement for the top while using the wand.

Your First Scene with the Wand

Make sure you have the wand power turned down before plugging it in. The knob at the base of the wand turns counter-clockwise to turn the power down, clockwise to turn the power up.

It's good to start with a round electrode to see how your partner will react to lighter sensations. Use a round light bulb or the mushroom probe to begin. I'd recommend trying these on yourself so you have some idea of how they will feel.

Don't spend too much time on one area, especially at first – different people have different reactions to the wand, and even a few minutes of relatively easy play can create a sunburn-like effect.

You'll notice that when the electrode is pressed against the body the sensations are barely noticeable – only when a bit of distance is created with the electricity arc and stimulate your partner.

From the round bulb or mushroom probe you can move on to the rake electrode or a smaller light bulb. Turn your power all the way down or off (if using a foot switch) before changing electrodes or you may surprise yourself. If using the rake, try moving it along the body with all the tines arcing, then just one or two – the difference in intensity should be felt by your partner.

Keep in mind that **where** you use the wand is just as important as what your power setting is. For example, a low power setting used on the arm will have a much different effect if used on the vagina.

After using direct mode for a while you can switch to indirect mode if you have a body contact probe.

With the probe on you are now the electrode, and can use anything from your hands, tongue, or kitchen utensils to conduct to your partner.

Other Wand Ideas to Try

✓ Conductive pipe brushes can be used solo or tied together to create all sorts of toys. They may also be wrapped around a vibrator or the top of a Hitachi Magic Wand to deliver electricity (I know I mentioned to keep the violet wand away from electronics previously, but I've used it with all sorts of vibrators and it hasn't prevented them from working)

✓ Spanking gains a new dimension while wearing the body contact probe, with your bare hands or anything conductive

✓ Dollar stores are good sources for violet wand toys. Metallic shred, forks, spoons, knives, egg whisks, pizza cutters, and many more fun toys may be had

✓ Metal objects may be placed in the freezer prior to use, creating a sort of "ice and fire" effect

✓ On a similar note, ice cubes can be rubbed over the skin prior to applying the wand. Watch out for small pools of water while doing this – they should be avoided

✓ The wand is fun to use with alcohol for fire play, but please make sure you are well-versed in fire play before attempting it

✓ Two or more bottoms may be connected to experience the wand, e.g. two people connect with wire – when the wand is applied to the wire both will feel it

✓ Some violet wand toys may be made at home, as we'll cover in the next section

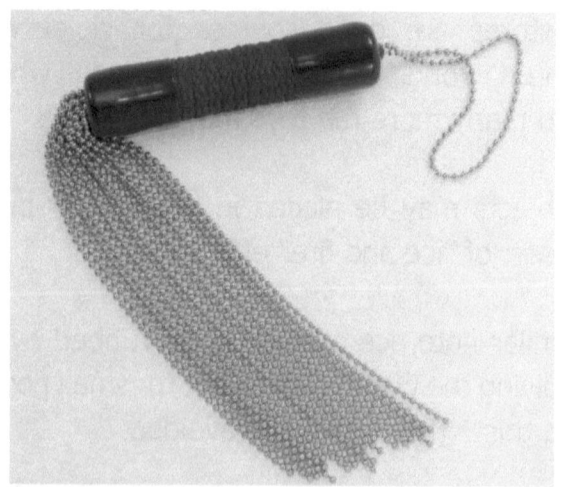

Chain flogger from prysmcreations.com

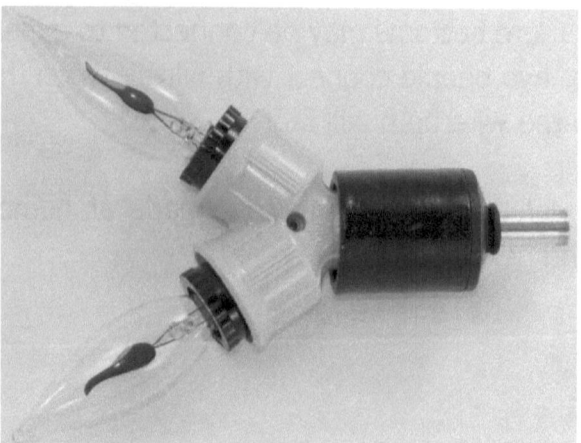

Two flicker flame candelabra bulbs with a light bulb splitter, connected with Edison adapter

Creating Your Own Wand Accessories

You can create an endless supply of wand accessories using copper tape, copper wire, or conductive pipe cleaners. The wire need not be copper, but it has a high conductivity so I'd recommend it.

With copper tape, which comes in several widths, you can electrify items like hairbrushes and paddles. Copper wire and conductive pipe cleaners may be wrapped around canes, bats, your hand, or used on their own.

Conductive paint can also be used to electrify items but don't try to use anything you've painted internally.

Cupping is a popular BDSM activity, and the cups may be electrified. Inexpensive plastic cupping sets can be made conductive with silver paint. Silver Print II was perfect for this but is apparently no longer being produced. Other copper or silver paints will work, but you need a thick paint so it doesn't flake off every time the pump is applied and removed from the top of the cup.

Use a box cutter to gently pry the valve off the top of the cup and apply the conductive paint inside and outside the area where the valve was. Once dried you can put it back together and the electricity from the wand will be able to travel through to the inside of the cup.

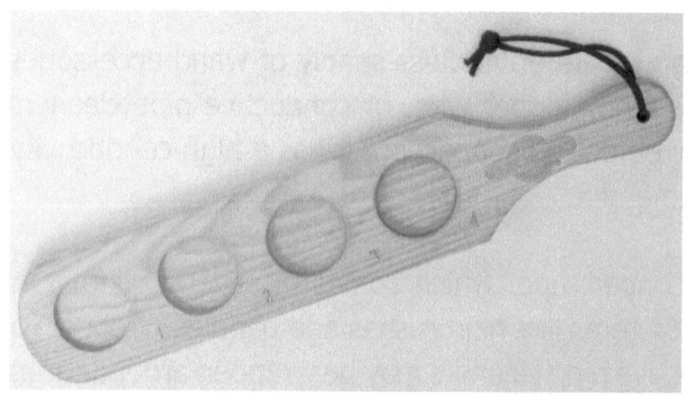

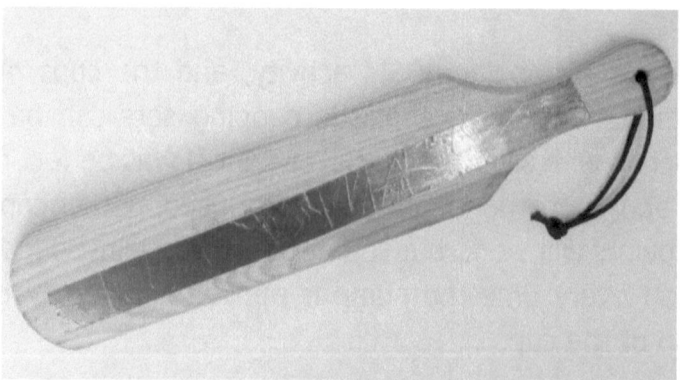

Wooden paddle made conductive with copper tape applied to one side.

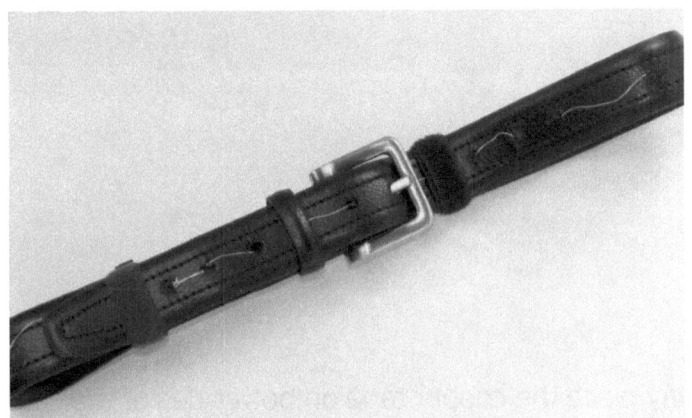

**A belt with wire woven through it to make it conductive.
Note sensations are intense with this due to
the thin gauge of the wire.**

Violet Wand Clothespins

The clothespin in this photo is 3.25″ long and the copper tape is .25″ wide (2.75″ long).

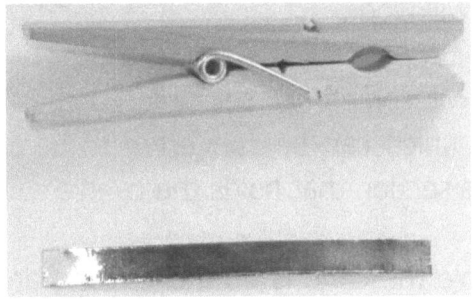

Place the tape on the clothespin, leaving a small amount of space at the end, so the electricity has room to arc to the skin:

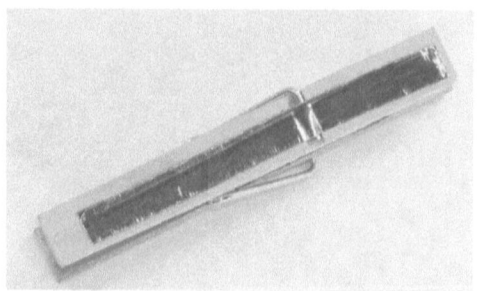

You may place the copper tape on both sides of the clothespin but since electricity will always take the shortest path it's difficult to get both sides to arc at the same time. Slowly moving the clothespin back and forth with whatever attachment you're using can produce good results.

Violet Wand Canes

To create a violet wand cane you will need a length of bamboo or other material for the cane, a length of wire, and a drill — any size drill bit wide enough to make a hole to push your wire through will work.

Dollar stores will sometimes sell "Tiki Torches" in the spring and summer which can be converted to bamboo canes by sawing off the section that holds the candle.

In this example the cane is 36 inches long and 2.75 inches around. The copper wire is 12 gauge and 80 inches long.

First, drill two holes into the bottom (whichever end you wish to hold onto) of the cane — drill them all the way through so you end up with four holes, 2 on each side, about 1" apart:

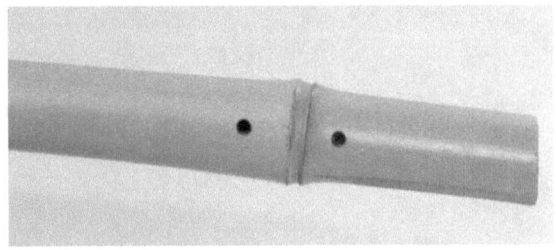

Next, drill one hole through the other end:

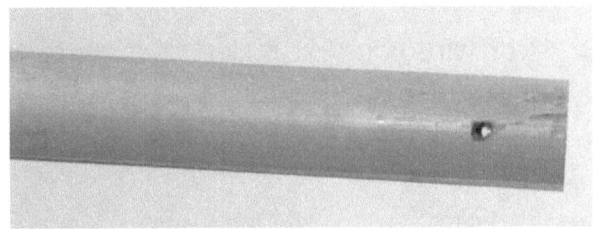

Then place about 3"-4" of the wire through the bottom hole:

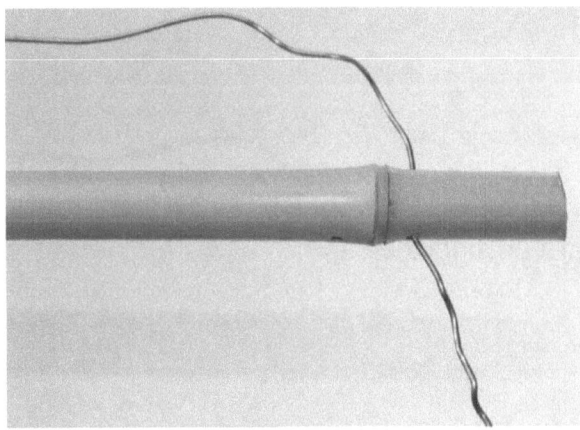

Take the rest of the wire and pull it through the hole immediately above. If you encounter resistance working with stiff wire pliers will help:

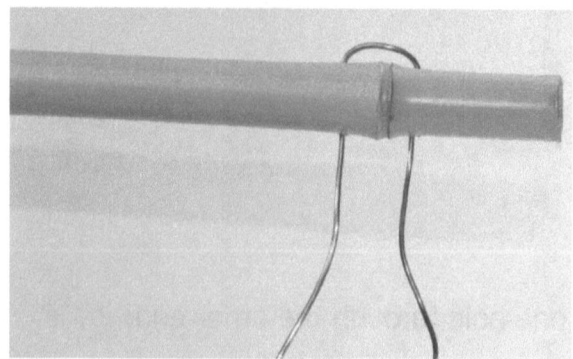

Use the 3"-4" of wire you first pulled through to tie off and secure the bottom:

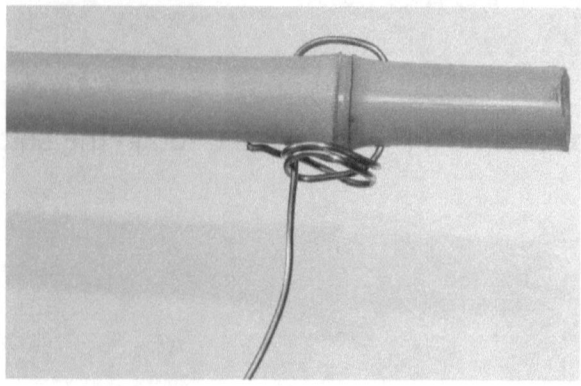

Coil the wire around the cane:

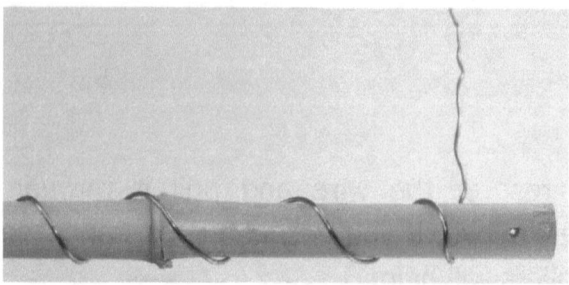

Pull the remaining wire through the top two holes:

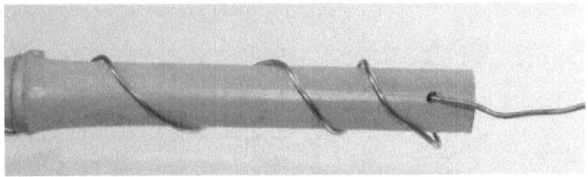

And secure any way you like. I prefer to bend the wire and cut it, leaving a sharp tip at the end:

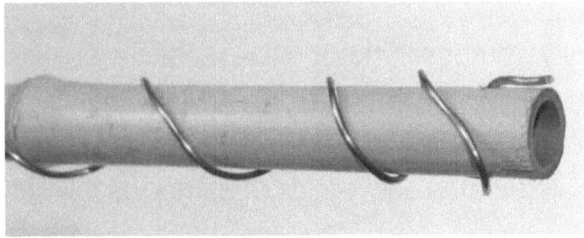

Stun Guns

Stun guns are electroshock weapons that use a temporary high-voltage low-current electrical discharge to override the body's muscle-triggering mechanisms. Application of the current is painful, and the person on the receiving end is likely to be momentarily paralyzed while the electric current is applied. Applying electroshock devices to more sensitive areas of the body is said to cause higher levels of pain.

For defensive purposes the most effective areas for stun gun usage are the upper shoulder, below the rib cage, and the upper hip. High voltages are used, but because most devices use a non-lethal current, death does not usually occur. The resulting "shock" is caused by muscles twitching uncontrollably, appearing as muscle spasms.

How Can You Use Stun Guns Safely?

It's not possible to be 100% safe when using a stun gun on someone. It is possible to be "safer" by screening potential play partners for issues, restricting where you stun them to certain areas (**avoid the darkened area in the illustration**), and exercising a higher than normal degree of caution during your scene.

Who Should Avoid Stun Gun Play?

Always make certain the person you are using a stun gun on does not have a pacemaker, diagnosed heartbeat problems, a history of heart attacks, or epilepsy, as in those cases a stun gun could cause problems - possibly fatal ones. Always avoid the spine when using a stun gun.

Volts and Amps

Stun guns are often advertised with very high voltage, but this should be considered hype.

The breakdown voltage of air is somewhat variable, but claiming hundreds of thousands of volts with only an inch or so between the terminals is impossible. Consider using low voltage (100,000 – 250,000v) stun guns since even the lower voltage models carry more than enough power to garner a reaction from your partner.

The amperage of stun guns is extremely low, which is good because 1/30th of an amp (30mA) can kill someone. Most stun guns only have between 5-8mA. That's enough to make a painful impression without doing any permanent damage.

How to Play With Stun Guns

✓ Everybody is different. The output current upon contact with the target will depend on various factors such as how new the battery is, the target's resistance, skin type, moisture, clothing, and the stun gun's internal circuitry.

✓ Be very careful with tight bondage. Stun guns will make someone spasm suddenly, so bondage that doesn't allow some wiggle room could harm them.

✓ The shock will be more intense if you power the device on prior to touching the skin, as opposed to resting it on the skin then turning it on.

✓ The shock may be reduced by increasing the size of the contact point (the metal electrodes at the end of the stun gun). Metal balls or nuts/bolts work well to increase the size of the contact point.

✓ Avoid prolonged contact (more than 2-3 seconds) in any one area. It's better to employ short jabs or quickly drag across the skin.

✓ Vaginal wetness can increase conductivity.

✓ Dollar store 9v batteries seldom work with stun guns. Use Energizer or Duracell batteries for best results.

✓ The stun gun doesn't always have to be the focal point of the scene. For instance, one or two brief shocks to the ass after a 20-30 minute beating can add a lot.

Video Glasses / Autoscopy

What Is Autoscopy?

Autoscopy is an experience in which the individual, while believing they are awake, sees his or her body from a position outside of their body. Stories of autoscopy have appeared in the folklore, spiritual narratives, and mythology of most ancient and modern societies. Modern psychiatrists frequently encounter cases of autoscopy.

Autoscopic experiences are characterized by the following three factors:

1. Disembodiment, an apparent location of the self outside one's body.

2. Impression of seeing the world from an elevated and distanced visuo-spatial perspective or extracorporeal, but egocentric visuo-spatial perspective.

3. Impression of seeing one's own body from this perspective (autoscopy)

The Laboratory of Cognitive Neuroscience in Geneva, Switzerland has studied cases of autoscopy and has stated that the precipitating factors in most cases are sleep, drug abuse, and general anesthesia as well as neurobiology. Researchers at the Laboratory have stated that experimental investigation of the mechanisms in autoscopies and related illusions in combination with neuroimaging and behavioral techniques might further our understanding of the central mechanisms of awareness and self-consciousness.

Autoscopy has also been linked to "new age" phenomena like out-of-body experiences and astral projection.

In my experience those who try the video glasses report the effects of the scene become more intense. For example, one lady who enjoyed wax play tried it with these and said that it was the first time she had an orgasm only from wax play and attributed that to being able to sit back and watch it.

Another common occurrence is a general feeling of being disoriented, and of "coming back" when removing the glasses after the scene.

How to Simulate Autoscopy

We can simulate autoscopy by using a head-mounted display, also known as "video glasses," in conjunction with video cameras.

Video glasses are worn like regular glasses, but they contain a small video screen (or screens) that allow the wearer to see any video signal input into the glasses.

I use the Vuzix Wrap 230 glasses with a rubber "light shield" that helps block out incoming light. These glasses are no longer in production but Vuzix and other companies like MyVu, EyeTop, and ITV make consumer-level video glasses.

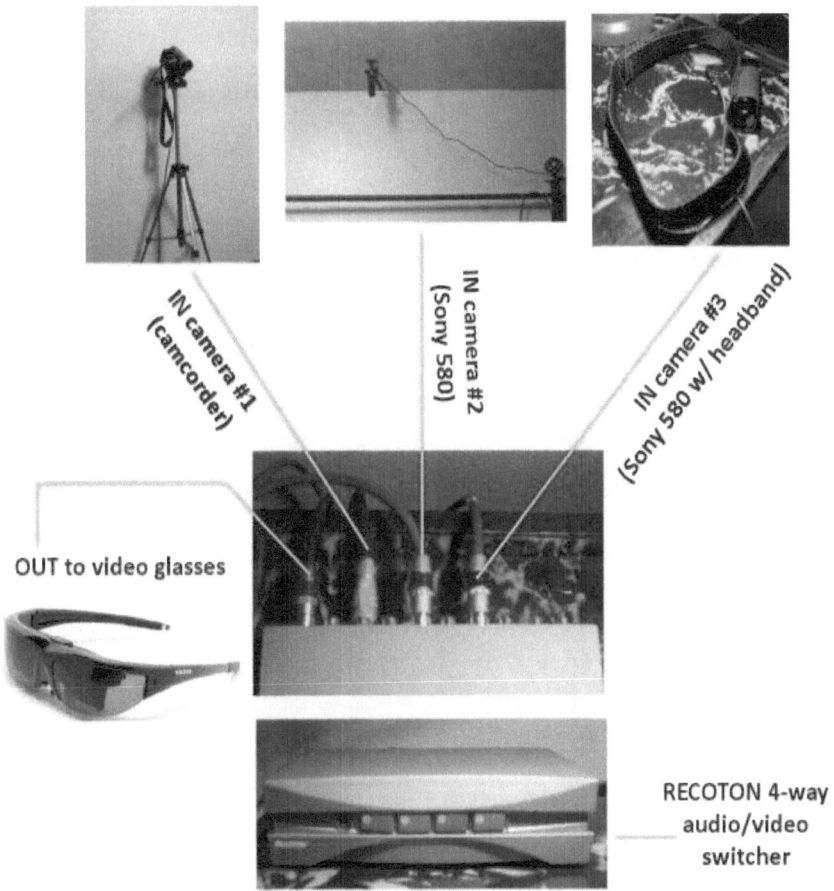

IN camera #1 (camcorder)

IN camera #2 (Sony 580)

IN camera #3 (Sony 580 w/ headband)

OUT to video glasses

RECOTON 4-way audio/video switcher

The Vuzix models usually come with RCA jack or "composite" inputs, the same inputs found on the back of almost all television receivers that are used to connect DVD players.

The easiest way to set up an autoscopy scene is to connect a camcorder that also has RCA jack inputs to the video glasses using a RCA cable. The camcorder can be placed on a tripod at the foot of the bed or other location. Newer camcorders may not have RCA inputs so some type of adapter may be necessary.

To create a more elaborate experience more cameras and an additional piece of equipment – an audio/video switcher – are needed.

The switcher allows you to input multiple video sources into the box, output the main signal to the video glasses, and switch between the sources by pressing the buttons on the front. You may also split the video output from the switcher between the video glasses and a small television, so the television acts as a "monitor" and allows you to see what is being viewed in the glasses at all times. Small Sony 580 helmet cameras can be used for the extra cameras – I have one mounted to the ceiling and an additional one I can wear around my head to let the bottom see things through "my eyes."

Additional Hints and Ideas:

If you already own RCA cables it's a good idea to buy some female/female RCA joiners – these let you connect multiple cables so you don't have to buy long ones.

Some of the scenes I've personally tried and had go well with video glasses are: wax, needles, fire, cutting, objectification, impact play, flogging, and the violet wand. The wand will interfere with the signal but it's still watchable.

You may input more than just live video into the glasses. With a DVD player connected to them you can have whoever is wearing the glasses watch porn, videos of themselves, or anything else.

The best place to buy equipment is almost always Ebay. RCA cables, joiners, Sony 580 cameras, and sometimes even switch boxes can be had at good prices.

Accessories that may enhance the experience are a special effects processor, mirrors surrounding the area, or a digital delay.

Having the bottom wear an eye patch will usually help them focus on one screen and may intensify the disorienting effect.

In the very near future augmented reality and virtual reality glasses will enhance play like video glasses can now.

Sources for video glasses are listed in the *Resources* section.

Resources

cpony.com/home/training/shockcollar.html
Slave Training with a Remote Training Collar by Master Gunter

currentpleasures.com
"Where Electric Becomes Erotic" – very good prices

drclockwork.com
Dr. Clockwork's Home for Electrical and Medical Oddities

electrastim.com
Electro Sex Toys & Erotic Electrostimulation

electricshock.org
The Electric Shock - A Powerful Force

E-stim.co.uk
E-Stim Systems – home of the 2B

fetishtoybox.com
giant selection of e-stim gear

happystim-usa.com
wide assortment of insertables, conductive rubber, and more

huse.com
Rupert Huse & Son, Inc - Tools for Controlling People –
e-stim and violet wand, plus stainless steel/acrylic
insertables and more

lhasaoms.com
Acupuncture supplies, great prices on accessories and pads

nickandmorphia.com
Modern, Classic & Vintage Violet Wands

nvidia.com
NVIDIA – video glasses & virtual reality glasses

peselectro.com
PES – Paradise Electro Stimulations – home of the PES box

shop.erostek.com
"We Bring You Pleasure ™" - ErosTek store with the 232,
302R, and 312

smartstim.com
a forum dedicated to e-stim – search for
"Davey Box" if you want to build your own inexpensive
music-driven e-stim device

stockroom.com
Top Quality Sex Toys & Bondage Gear Since 1989

store.e-stimsystems.com
E-Stim Systems Store, Professional Electro Stimulation with the personal touch

violetwand.com
news and reviews

violetwand.org
Violet Wand Informational Resource Page, by Huse & Son

violetwanda.net
Violet Wanda's site, wands and electrodes for sale

violetwands.org
International Violet Wand Guild

violetwandstore.com
wand kits, accessories, and more

vuzix.com
"View the Future" - video glasses

xtremerestraints.com
Extreme Restraints

zeiss.com/cinemizer-oled/en_us/home.html
Carl Zeiss - Cinemizer video glasses

FetLife Groups:

(An account at FetLife.com is necessary to view these)

SAFE Electro Play
fetlife.com/groups/11210

Dr. Clockwork's Home for Electrical and Medical Oddities
fetlife.com/groups/3755

Electrical play
fetlife.com/groups/210

Electrical Play/Stim Medical/Accident Reports
fetlife.com/groups/1172

electro fun
fetlife.com/groups/5025

electro 'torture'
fetlife.com/groups/6286

International Violet Wand Guild
fetlife.com/groups/15741

Tens Unit, Violet Wands and all things electric
fetlife.com/groups/278

The Remote-Control Devices Group
fetlife.com/groups/14638

Violet Wand Developments, Tech and Culture
fetlife.com/groups/51003

Violet Wand
fetlife.com/groups/6311

Inexpensive Toys & Accessories:

Check eibon.us for updates to this list, wholesalers come and go frequently.

tinyurl.com/l2wt2ze
Bipolar vaginal probe for $9.85

tinyurl.com/pqyfhsm
Five Liberty Probes (pictured on page 51) for $73.43 – less than $15/each

tinyurl.com/o38hvtu
Assortment of probes – 2 anal, 3 vaginal – for $92

tinyurl.com/oa5ystd
Ten 2.5mm female -> 3.5mm male adapters for $5.49

tinyurl.com/k5tvsja
3.5mm male to TENS pins wires for $1.15

tinyurl.com/ky5q8vj

3.5mm male to snap connectors, $25.90 for 20

tinyurl.com/pyue8ww

30 TENS pads for $9.20

Photo / Illustration Credits

Pages:

Cover - **Placitas, New Mexico Lightning by John Fowler**

19 (1st) - **E. Price Edwards, page 94 of *Our Seamarks***

19 (2nd), 26, 50-53, 63, 92-95, 100, 102-107 – **Rysyn - fetlife.com/users/578648**

29, 31, 44, 58 – **ElectraStim**

24, 73 - **PES**

33, 42 - **E-stim Systems**

35, 37, 46 - **ErosTek**

39 – **Steffen**

88-89 – **Renulife Violet Ray manual**

113 - **author**

About the Author

After spending several years living in Europe while serving in the US military Eibon returned to the States and began an informal study of the dark side of the mind, which consisted of everything from managing "Mystery" of VH1's "The Pickup Artist" fame to studying the linguistic stylings of Charles Manson. A late-night encounter with a young woman he met online in late 2005 piqued his curiosity about BDSM. In 2006 he officially entered the scene, then by late 2007 he had purchased his first electrical gear and was off and running, giving demonstrations not too long after.

Known for bearing a sadistic grin and frequently accused of "evil" he is a member of the Society of Janus, was a Founder in the Boise BDSM Society, created the "Idaho BDSM" group on FetLife, maintains IdahoBDSM.com, has had his writing appear in SECRET Magazine from Belgium, and appeared in shadow to talk about the lifestyle with Boise CBS affiliate KBOI-2 for their "A Little 50 Shades - Boise Style" feature in May 2013. His presentations range from the serious to the absurd, often reflecting the energy of the audience.

One attendee said of him: "*You have an intensity that keeps me glued to my seat and forgetting to breathe. :)*"

In addition to doing presentations in and around his home in Boise he's also presented for the following groups/events:

Adventures in Sexuality: C.O.P.E. – Columbus, Ohio
Frolicon 2015 – Atlanta, Georgia
Kinkfest 2015 – Portland, Oregon
Madtown Kinkfest – Madison, Wisconsin
Sin in the City – Las Vegas, Nevada
SF Citadel Community Center - San Francisco, California
Northern Exposure G4 – Anchorage, Alaska
Arizona Power Exchange (APEX) – Phoenix, Arizona
Behind Closed Doors 5 – Tucson, Arizona
The Group in Fresno – Fresno, California
Lair de Sade - North Hollywood, California
Paradise Unbound – Seattle, Washington
Naughty Knoxville – Knoxville, Tennessee

If you'd like Eibon to present at your event please contact him at **eibon76@gmail.com**

Visit **www.eibon.us** for a complete list of available presentations.

FetLife: fetlife.com/users/11842
Twitter: twitter.com/_Eibon_